How to Decorate

CLARKSON POTTER/PUBLISHERS

NEW YORK

Originally published in book form
by Time Warner in 1996.
Published simultaneously
by Clarkson N. Potter, Inc.,
Oxmoor House, Inc., and Leisure Arts.

The photographs in this work were
previously published in
MARTHA STEWART LIVING.

Published by Clarkson N. Potter, Inc.,
201 East 50th Street
New York, New York 10022.
Member of the Crown Publishing Group.

Random House, Inc. New York, Toronto,
London, Sydney, Auckland.

Clarkson N. Potter, Potter, and colophon
are trademarks of Clarkson N. Potter, Inc.

Manufactured in the
United States of America.
Library of Congress
Cataloguing-in-Publication
is available upon request.
ISBN 0-517-88780-0

Creative Director: Gael Towey
Designer: Constance Old
Writer: Celia Barbour
Editor: Eugenia Leftwich
Managing Editor: Amy Schuler
Style Director: Stephen Earle

Contents

Introduction

WHEN I WAS GROWING UP IN OUR FAMILY'S MODEST TWO-STORY, THREE-BEDROOM home in Nutley, New Jersey, neither the idea nor the reality of interior decoration was of great importance. The eight of us Kostyras were more concerned with finding a comfortable place to study in and an adequate spot in which to sleep.

The house was serviceable, crowded, and clean, but pretty much devoid of style—primarily because of a great paucity of money. My handsome father had grand dreams that far exceeded his finances, and besides, he preferred to spend whatever leisure time he had in the garden. Mother had no time to sew curtains or faux-paint walls—she was too busy cooking and sewing clothes for her six children.

It was not until I married the son of a very talented decorator that I felt an urge to beautify my surroundings. In college, I began to study the decorative arts and architecture and—taking a cue from my father, a fine colorist—color theory and application. Our first apartment was furnished mostly with hand-me-downs, but our second apartment, seven rooms overlooking the Hudson River, was a reflection of my new interest—with milk-chocolate-brown walls, shiny white trim, unusual velvets, brown glazed chintzes, and English furniture found at auctions and sales. This was the first of my forays into an art form that has become for me a passion.

What I have learned, after designing and decorating five homes, is that decorating is something one can learn to do, that it consists of the ability to turn a space, however small, into a home that is inviting, warm, and useful. And while it can mean putting everything one deems beautiful into a space, it can also be a process of editing out everything unnecessary.

This book is intended to give you insight into the fascinating world of decorating. Most of the material was designed by the talented contributors to and staff of MARTHA STEWART LIVING magazine. I hope it will guide you in developing your own decorating talent.

Martha Stewart

Color

It is a luxury to live with beautiful color, to give your eyes the continual pleasure of absorbing rich and subtle shades from your surroundings. It's also one of the easiest decorating projects you can undertake, for a simple coat of paint is within reach of

nearly everyone, and has truly transformative powers. Yet in order for a color palette to really work in your home, it has to meet a variety of criteria, from the sentimental to the scientific. Getting it right isn't a mystery, however; it's a simple matter of learning how to open your eyes to the nuances of color.

Eve Ashcraft, a paint and color specialist in New York City, has developed a list of questions to help her clients choose colors. It's not a test; many of the questions don't even provoke clear-cut answers. "What this does is get someone to begin thinking about color," she says.

WHAT IS THE ROOM USED FOR? In rooms where you won't spend much time, such as powder rooms or entrance halls, you can get away with dramatic colors that would become tiresome in living spaces. Rooms with a multitude of purposes should be painted a versatile neutral.

HOW BIG IS THE ROOM? Dark colors create a sense of intimacy appropriate to small spaces; lighter colors provide the ease and openness that large rooms require.

HOW DO YOU WANT THE ROOM TO FEEL? AND HOW DO YOU WANT TO FEEL IN THE ROOM? These questions are tricky, says Ashcraft. "People often say they want a soft room or a cozy room, but if you need to be thinking and working, you don't want colors that are too sleepy." Asking yourself how you want a room to feel is as important as determining how you want it to look, since color isn't simply a visual phenomenon—it also has great emotional power. Studies have found that colors affect people's judgment and reactions: Blue is a sedative and can calm anxious nerves, red and other warm colors make time seem to move more slowly, and yellow improves students'

OPPOSITE A deep, intense color like Gaillardia Red comes alive in warm lamplight but may seem murky by day, so it works well in a bedroom. The chintz quilt is from the 1850s. (Our palettes appear on pages 28 and 31.)

grades. But there are no hard-and-fast rules; the world is full of calm brick reds and anxious neon blues.

WHAT KIND OF LIGHTING DOES THE ROOM HAVE? Light activates color, and can change its character dramatically. The warm glow of incandescent lamps will give some colors a golden flush and cause others to turn sour. Halogen lamps can neutralize and flatten colors. Lampshades add another layer of color to light. "If you have red silk lampshades and pea-green walls," says Ashcraft, "you're going to have a muddy cast where the light hits the wall."

WHAT TIME OF DAY OR NIGHT DO YOU MOST USE THE ROOM? The quality of light changes throughout the course of the day, from pink and lilac in the morning, to lemon yellow at midday, to the deep, rich gold of evening. Ashcraft tells her clients to look carefully at their walls and describe how many colors they see; it's often possible to distinguish as many as a dozen as the light plays across the surfaces and reflects off of nearby objects.

HOW MANY WINDOWS ARE THERE, AND WHAT ARE THEIR EXPOSURES? Within the same house, the rooms facing north will be filled with a bluer, cooler light than rooms with a

Drabware, a glazed English earthenware (shown above and displayed on the wall at left), inspired the wall color in this dining room. Because this neutral is so complex and highly pigmented, it works in almost any color scheme. Here, Silkie White was used on the woodwork, and an entirely different hue—Araucana Turquoise—on the ceiling for contrast and surprise.

southern exposure. The only way to find out how a color will behave on the walls is to swatch-test it in the room you're planning to paint (see "Light and Color," page 30). WHAT ARE THE PREDOMINANT COLORS OF THE FURNITURE, WINDOW TREATMENTS, FLOOR, OR FLOOR COVERING? Most people aren't starting from scratch when they paint. Your color choices are probably limited by the upholstery, carpets, and artwork you already own. Look to these things for inspiration, but avoid reading the cues too literally. Rather than matching a blue in the upholstery or carpet exactly, for example, find a blue paint color that's softer and richer, with gray or an earth pigment added to it. The interplay of these slightly mismatched colors will create a less static environment in the room. When furnishings are a crazy quilt of colors, it's tempting to cling to the safety of white walls. But white is seldom the most satisfying solution. "People think that white makes the most neutral background," says Stephen Earle, style director of MARTHA STEWART LIVING. "But it actually makes any other color jump out at you. If you want to neutralize a room, find a color that blends the things together."

WHAT COLORS DO YOU LIKE? WHAT COLORS DO YOU NOT LIKE? People have strong prejudices about color: They may claim to despise brown, for example, and refuse even to consider it. But sometimes the fault isn't with the color at all; it's a negative association conjured up by the name. "If I call a mud color 'Café au Lait,'" says Ashcraft, "all of a sudden you're in Paris having a blast."

ARE THERE PICTURES OR PLACES THAT INSPIRE YOU? If nothing comes to mind, take the time to look around. Go to museums and historic houses; look at architecture and design books; go to decorators' showrooms. You'll start noticing combinations that appeal to you and others that make your hair stand on end. You don't have to be totally original when painting your rooms. There is so much beautiful color in the world already, and you're free to copy it.

After answering these questions, some general guidelines should begin to appear. But it's still essential to fine-tune color choices. Two colors that look nearly identical on a paint chip can behave completely differently on the walls. The variation is often due to the number of pigments included in the blend. Most paints are a mixture of two or three pigments softened by the addition of white or gray. Highly pigmented paints, on the other hand, begin with the same amount of the dominant pigment, but also contain a wide range of other pigments. On the wall, these paints are full of nuances, appearing alive and mutable as they reveal hidden shades of character during the course of a day. For an inveterate collector like Martha Stewart, such complex colors provide the perfect backdrop to an ever-changing assortment of objects, since they harmonize with almost anything. "The drabware color in my New York apartment is so effective," she says. "I can alter the color scheme whenever I find new fabrics, antiques, accessories."

In the end, there's just one surefire method of finding out how a color will look when it's painted in a room. "People have to be brave enough to buy a few test quarts and put them up and look at them for twenty-four hours," says Ashcraft. "It's the only way to really know. You can't take a color aside and examine it any more than you can take a note out of a symphony and decide if it's a good or bad note. Context is everything." And when that context is your home, the right color can bring it all into beautiful harmony.

OPPOSITE The paint colors in the butler's pantry of Martha Stewart's East Hampton house—Thyme Flower Mauve on the ceiling and Pansy Brown on the walls—were chosen to complement its handcrafted mahogany woodwork. The nineteenth-century pendant lamp from Ceylon and cool white marble countertops continue the British colonial feeling.

OPPOSITE With its rough pine floors, whitewashed French side chairs, and softly colored walls, this living room has the calm, spare feeling of a Gustavian Swedish interior. The walls are painted Araucana Sage, the ceiling Araucana Blue—quietly intense colors that serve as foils to the milky-white furnishings, which would fade in an all-white room. Walls that are perfectly smooth and true like these can be painted with a satin finish, which creates a reflective surface that captures both daylight and lamplight. It is also easier to clean than a matte finish. However, satin paint highlights blemishes and shouldn't be used on rough walls. THIS PAGE In the formal dining room of Martha's Federal-style house in Westport, Connecticut, dinner guests are enveloped by vivid color. Lively and intense colors are well suited to small rooms such as this, where people don't spend great lengths of time. The French cut-crystal chandelier and gilded acanthus-leaf mirror make light sparkle across the walls. The Hepplewhite chairs are upholstered in Scalamandré silk. Martha felt free to use colors like this in her own interiors after historical research revealed that paint colors of the Federal period were brighter than had been previously thought. This Porcelain Green was inspired by an antique Royal Doulton bowl; the ceiling color, Coral Blue Guinea, came from a length of silk ribbon.

The deep blue walls and green floor and ceiling of this bedroom appear to merge at the edges, blurring the room's corners and giving it a weightless quality. An Empire bedside table and 1930s bed were painted in white enamel. Light floods in through the tops of Gothic-revival windows over dotted-swiss half-curtains. The blue on a 1940s map (left) was matched for the wall color, Oceana; eggs from Martha's exotic chickens inspired the Araucana Olive floor and Pale Araucana Green ceiling. OPPOSITE Strong colors needn't intimidate; when carefully balanced, they create a satisfying harmony. The colors of Martha's Westport dressing room were inspired by her wardrobe—a good place for anyone to begin looking for colors she can live with. The walls are painted Crevecoeur, a dark brown that works well in small doses. Here it's relieved by cabinets in Golden Campine, a yellow with flattering peach undertones. The ceiling is Pale Araucana Green.

OPPOSITE Using bright colors is a risk worth taking in small, private spaces, like this children's guest room in Martha's East Hampton house, painted Larkspur Pink. The strong vertical lines of a French wrought-iron bed are repeated in the rhythm of the beaded-board woodwork and add graphic contrast to the sweetness of this old-fashioned color. THIS PAGE A color should fit into the overall plan for a home, so that moving from room to room is a fluid experience, filled with subtle changes but no jarring surprises. The Araucana Turquoise, Ameraucana Buff, and Araucana Sage used here are variations on neighboring colors from the color wheel: blue, yellow, and green. Using a single color for the woodwork helps unify the spaces.

Subtle shading calls out the architectural details of the living room above, which include a large plaster cornice and a picture rail below it. Partridge Rock Brown was used on the ceiling, Ameraucana Wheaten on the soffit, Salmon Faverolle on the walls (shown more closely opposite, bottom right). Using color to articulate the moldings of a room is an idea borrowed from the work of Robert Adam, a British architect of the eighteenth century. Because the room receives strong natural light and the ceiling is quite high, the dark ceiling appears comforting rather than oppressive. A light ceiling recedes (opposite, top left). Painting it a peachy beige, such as Buff Cochin, instead of stark white, softens the contrast with the putty-colored walls. Pale, ethereal blues and greens (opposite, bottom left), are traditional colors for ceilings, since they evoke the sky. Because a colored ceiling will reflect a cool light downward, wall color should be selected to complement it, and the two should be swatch-tested side by side to ensure that the interplay between them isn't jarring. Ceiling color can also be used to draw the eye to dramatic light fixtures. Martha selected the colors for a coffered ceiling (opposite top right) to set off a teal 1920s Venetian-glass chandelier. The recessed panels of her East Hampton library are painted Eucalyptus Green, the beams high-gloss Hosta Green.

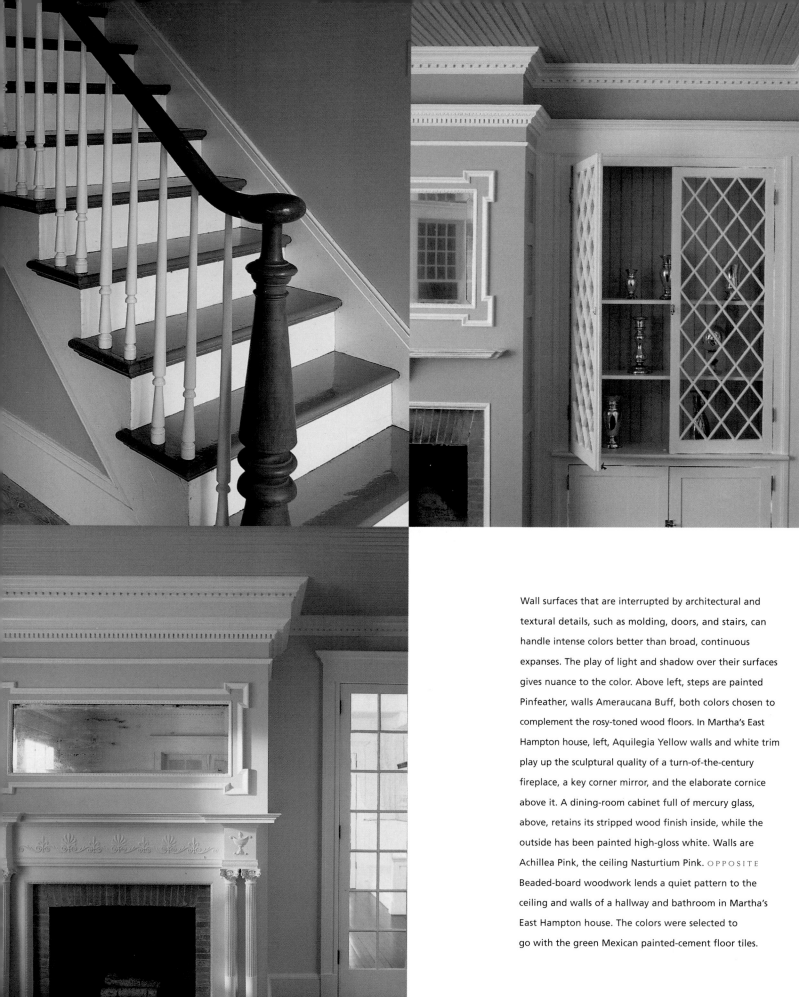

Wall surfaces that are interrupted by architectural and textural details, such as molding, doors, and stairs, can handle intense colors better than broad, continuous expanses. The play of light and shadow over their surfaces gives nuance to the color. Above left, steps are painted Pinfeather, walls Ameraucana Buff, both colors chosen to complement the rosy-toned wood floors. In Martha's East Hampton house, left, Aquilegia Yellow walls and white trim play up the sculptural quality of a turn-of-the-century fireplace, a key corner mirror, and the elaborate cornice above it. A dining-room cabinet full of mercury glass, above, retains its stripped wood finish inside, while the outside has been painted high-gloss white. Walls are Achillea Pink, the ceiling Nasturtium Pink. OPPOSITE Beaded-board woodwork lends a quiet pattern to the ceiling and walls of a hallway and bathroom in Martha's East Hampton house. The colors were selected to go with the green Mexican painted-cement floor tiles.

Architectural details can be created with color, even if they don't already exist. A subtle horizon line divides this mudroom wall; the lower half of the wall is painted Ameraucana Moss in a satin finish for easier cleanup, the upper half is Araucana Olive in matte. The floor is Araucana Teal, with a durable high-gloss finish. OPPOSITE Warm southern light floods the front hall of Martha's East Hampton house, where two tempered beiges—Liatris White on walls and Lunaria White on the ceiling—emphasize the room's formal style. The softly colored walls seem to recede, bringing the woodwork into the foreground and drawing attention to furnishings, like a Victorian Eastlake-style chair with needlepoint cushions. As this hall illustrates, an all-white room needn't be monotonous. It gains distinction and depth when painted a palette of contrasting warm and cool whites.

ARAUCANA BLUE

ARAUCANA GREEN

ARAUCANA SAGE

BUFF COCHIN

PINFEATHER

PUTTY

AMERAUCANA BUFF

PALE ARAUCANA GREEN

ARAUCANA TURQUOISE

OCEANA

DRABWARE

ARAUCANA OLIVE

SILKIE WHITE

AMERAUCANA MOSS

CREVECOEUR

ARAUCANA TEAL

GOLDEN CAMPINE

PARTRIDGE ROCK BROWN

PORCELAIN GREEN

AMERAUCANA WHEATEN

CORAL BLUE GUINEA

SALMON FAVEROLLE

The Araucana Colors, inspired by the delicate hues of the eggs laid by
Martha's Araucana and Ameraucana chickens, are subtle mixes of
many pigments. For information about the color chart for this palette
or for Colors From the Garden, shown on page 31, see The Guide.

About paint

The basic formula for making paint hasn't changed
since the Egyptians painted the tombs inside their pyra-
mids red, green, and blue five thousand years ago.
Now, as then, paint consists of solid pigments ground
to a powder and suspended in a viscous liquid carrier,
or "vehicle." The vehicle evenly coats a surface with
microscopic grains of pigment and then evaporates,
leaving behind a colorful protective film. The Greeks
used egg white, glue, and honey as vehicles; early
American painters sometimes used buttermilk. Today
the most commonly used vehicles consist of either veg-
etable oils, resins, and solvents (in oil-based paint) or
resins and water (in water-based, or latex, paint).
Modern vehicles also contain additives to speed drying,
prevent mildewing, and improve surface appearance.

A few of the pigments used today occur naturally in
mineral form, but most are produced chemically and
are known as synthetics. Synthetic colors are more var-
ied than earthen colors and more transparent, giving
greater luminosity to paint. Natural pigments have
excellent hiding properties and subtle, complex hues.
They include ochers, siennas, umbers, and oxides.

Although oil-based and latex paints share many of
the same ingredients, they perform a bit differently.
Because oil-based paint contains solvents, it releases
smelly toxic fumes as it dries and requires cleanup with
mineral spirits. It is also more water resistant than latex
(a plus in kitchens and bathrooms); it adheres more easily to rough or deteriorated surfaces; and it can be
applied more successfully at temperatures below sixty
degrees. Latex paint is odorless, can be cleaned up with
soap and water, and dries faster than oil.

Both types of paint are available in a range of finishes: flat, or matte; slightly glossier eggshell; semigloss,
or satin; and high gloss. Traditionally, a flat finish is
used on ceilings, flat or eggshell on walls, and semigloss
on trim. High gloss paint must be used sparingly—it
highlights any surface imperfection.

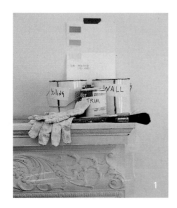

HOW TO PAINT A ROOM

Before you begin painting, you must choose the most crucial item—the paint itself. This is not the place to scrimp; buy the finest quality you can afford. Paint and color specialist Eve Ashcraft recommends oil-based paint for trim and floors because of its long life and durability. (She often uses water-soluble latex on ceilings and walls because it dries in about half the time.) To make the job easier, assemble the following supplies: a solvent (for oil-based paint); paint trays, rollers, and sleeves; a roller extension; several natural-bristle brushes (4" for large areas, 2½" for trim, and 1½" for narrow trim); a utility knife; painter's blue masking tape and duct tape; sandpaper; a painter's cap; a brush spinner; and a 5-in-1 tool that's handy for everything from scraping to opening cans. 1 Cans and lids should be labeled— ceiling, wall, trim—to show where the paint will go. 2 Building paper is spread over the floor to protect it from spills. Low-adhesive blue tape holds the paper together and doesn't leave marks on surfaces. (For wall-to-wall carpeting, you'll need a heavier cover: sheets of 4-mil-plastic are a good choice. Use blue tape around the perimeter and more-adhesive duct tape to attach

the plastic to blue tape and to join the sheets together.) 3 Screws from electrical plates and other hardware are taped together and labeled to avoid confusion. 4 After sanding, dust surfaces with a damp cotton rag or a brush. The next step is to apply the primer. If using oil-based paint over an old latex job, use oil-based primer, and vice versa. After it dries, go over primer quickly and lightly with fine sandpaper. 5 Use a paint-brush to paint in corners; while the paint is wet, fill in the walls with a roller, overlapping the brushed-on areas. 6 An extension pole attached to a roller makes the job easier. 7 Although some painters mask around window trim before painting, Ashcraft advises against it, because tape can leak. Instead, she paints the trim as neatly as possible, lets it dry, then removes excess paint with a scraper. 8 Since a paint job may take several days, materials must be kept in shape overnight. Store paint-saturated roller sleeves in airtight plastic bags. Clean brushes in mineral spirits using the brush spinner, then wash in detergent, rinse, and reshape. (Cleanup for latex paint is simpler: just clean tools with warm water and soap, and wipe up spills with wet cloths.)

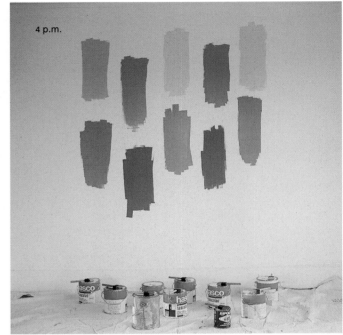

LIGHT AND COLOR

The only way to select a paint color that will really work is to test swatches of it on the walls to be painted. Light animates color, and can change it dramatically depending on how it fills a room. Very bright colors look best in the tropics, for example, where blinding sunlight washes out even the most saturated hues. But the vivid turquoises, tangerines, and flamingo pinks that seem so cheerful in Miami Beach can look garish further north, where sunlight is diluted by the atmosphere, allowing colors to shine with greater intensity. Latitude isn't the only factor affecting the quality of light, however. Within the same house, the rooms facing north will be filled with a bluer, cooler light than rooms with a southern exposure.

Light is also affected by the other surfaces it reflects off of. A room with a gray-blue flagstone floor will take on a very different cast than one with yellowish pine floorboards. Light that passes through a canopy of trees will pick up a greenish tinge before coming through a window. The quality of light also changes throughout the course of the day, from morning lilac to evening gold.

We tested several pinks in bold swatches to see how they would look at different times of day. The swatches at left are shown at 9 A.M. in an east-facing room. By 4 P.M. (right), they have lost some of their glow. If a room will be used primarily at night, test colors in artificial light. Incandescent light is much yellower than sunlight; fluorescent is white and tends to sap a color's warmth.

Swatching several paints at once helps you compare colors that appear similar seen individually. Side by side, their differences emerge: one reveals itself to be cooler, another warmer, yet another shows a greenish undertone.

Don't be conservative when swatching paints; apply patches at least two feet square. Apply them on several walls—next to a window to see them in bright light, and in a corner as well. Color reflects off itself, and where two walls meet is intensified and becomes more vibrant.

To test colors to be used for trim, prime a piece of plywood and paint it with the sample color. It can then be moved from room to room and checked in various illuminations and in combination with colors used on the walls.

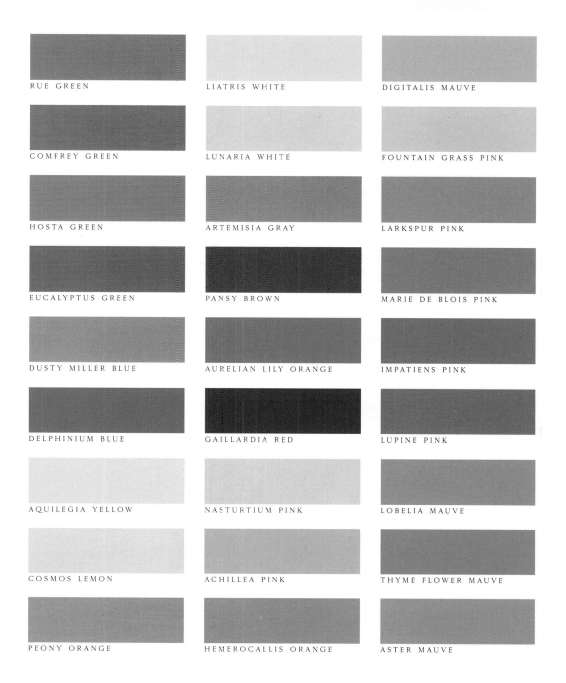

RUE GREEN	LIATRIS WHITE	DIGITALIS MAUVE
COMFREY GREEN	LUNARIA WHITE	FOUNTAIN GRASS PINK
HOSTA GREEN	ARTEMISIA GRAY	LARKSPUR PINK
EUCALYPTUS GREEN	PANSY BROWN	MARIE DE BLOIS PINK
DUSTY MILLER BLUE	AURELIAN LILY ORANGE	IMPATIENS PINK
DELPHINIUM BLUE	GAILLARDIA RED	LUPINE PINK
AQUILEGIA YELLOW	NASTURTIUM PINK	LOBELIA MAUVE
COSMOS LEMON	ACHILLEA PINK	THYME FLOWER MAUVE
PEONY ORANGE	HEMEROCALLIS ORANGE	ASTER MAUVE

CUSTOMIZING COLORS This palette was custom-mixed to match a faded chart of flower colors in an old gardening book that Martha found at an antiques fair. Why bother custom mixing colors? Most store-bought paints don't have much depth or complexity. They contain two or three pigments, plus white or gray to soften the color. In custom mixing, various pigments are used instead of gray to tone down the dominant color without sapping the life out of it. Gael Towey, creative director of MARTHA STEWART LIVING, always asks paint salesmen how many pigments are in a blend, and will request that they add other pigments to enrich it. One simple way to deepen a color is to add a touch of its opposite on the color wheel. A color wheel, which can be bought at a paint store, is the spectrum (red, orange, yellow, green, blue, and violet) displayed as a circle. The three primary colors, red, blue, and yellow, are separated by the colors produced when they are combined; for example, between blue and yellow is green, a mixture of the two. Green added to pink (a variation of red, green's opposite) will mellow its sweetness without dulling it. Highly pigmented paints that are as rich as any custom-mixed colors do exist; the brands that identify themselves as full-spectrum tend to be top quality and quite expensive. Their effect, though subtle, is extraordinary.

Martha Stewart wanted to be able to move seamlessly between the roles of cook and hostess in her New York apartment, so she planned what she calls her "galley alley" to make it possible. With the door open, there's no barrier between the kitchen and dining room. Now she can talk with dinner guests while preparing a meal. To make the most of the limited space, she had it outfitted with metal cabinets and equipment from Duralab, a company that custom manufactures laboratory furniture. The streamlined kitchen appears elegant and efficient rather than clinical, so it doesn't clash with the dining room beyond, where a French Consulat Cuban-mahogany pedestal table is surrounded by 1940s tubular metal chairs. The table setting is equally eclectic: contemporary Japanese ceramic bowls and chopsticks are combined with Indian silver cups and eighteenth-century English silverware.

Gathering

How to create a welcoming environment in every room of the house

INVITING FRIENDS TO GATHER TOGETHER UNDER OUR ROOFS IS AN ancient impulse, and a satisfaction familiar to every host. But in order for your home to feel warm to others, it has to please you and your family first. If your rooms are designed for the approval of some imaginary visitor, you wind up with "dead space"—formal rooms that sit around awaiting events that seldom come to pass, the rooms people pass by on their way to someplace more comfortable. To bring such spaces back to life, ask yourself how you really use each one, or long to use it; how you want it to feel, not what you want it to look like. The fact is, most people's lifestyles have evolved beyond the limitations implied by the traditional room names: You may dine in the kitchen and take dessert in the parlor; "live" in the family room, and use the living room as a kind of quiet study.

Draw inspiration and decorating ideas from the spots you use most now: the comfortable chair where you talk on the phone, the sunny corner of the kitchen where you share coffee with friends. Figure out what combination of good lighting, comfort, and practicality makes these places work and apply the same criteria to other rooms.

Once you have created a welcoming environment, accommodating others is simply a matter of keeping some things flexible—a surprisingly old-fashioned idea. Before 1800, most rooms were furnished with lightweight tables and chairs that were pushed against the walls until needed for tea or cards. Though most furniture arrangements now permanently inhabit the middle of our rooms, it's still wise to have a few movable pieces on the sidelines that can be brought forth or rearranged as events—or seasons—dictate. Resist the impulse to fill every inch of floor space with furniture. A balance of open space and coziness leaves room for movement and change, making a home feel as alive and vital as the friends and family who gather there.

OPPOSITE Vintage bar stools invite guests to gather around a kitchen counter while meals are being prepared in this open-plan cottage. Their bright vinyl tops echo the mood of the interior, which owner Alexis Stewart describes as a "happy soda shop." Alexis, Martha's daughter, renovated the 1870s carriage house in 1990 to showcase objects she acquired during a two-month drive across the country. Her extensive collections of housewares from the 1930s through the 1950s spills over from the kitchen to become part of the decor in other areas. Jade-ite Fire King dinnerware, made by the Anchor Hocking Glass Company, fills a tall open shelf overlooking the living area. Fifties bamboo chairs have been given a fresh coat of glossy white paint and upholstered with vintage awning fabric.

ABOVE An enamel-topped kitchen table from the 1930s has fold-out leaves to handle up to six guests. Alexis ignores the boundary between collectible and usable, setting her table with the same vintage housewares that line the walls. LEFT Before designing the cottage, Alexis inventoried the "boxes and boxes" of things she had collected, then roughed out how much shelf space she would need to hold it all. Shelves beneath the kitchen island were created to show off her Anchor Hocking Banded Rings glassware. Five years later, Alexis sold off every piece of this vintage tableware at a giant yard sale and completely redesigned the carriage house. Like her mother, she approaches interior design with a sense of freedom and creativity, and won't hesitate to change a space that no longer suits her style. See page 45 for a picture of the current interior.

ABOVE When work carries over into private life, housekeeping can suffer. For Magrino, books are a professional as well as a private passion, however, and something she's proud to show off. OPPOSITE Light, mobile chairs are easy to rearrange. The shapes of the furnishings are interesting but the palette is neutral—a combination that makes the interior a lively place to welcome company but also a peaceful respite from a hectic life.

Even a small city apartment can accommodate a wide variety of social events. Publicist Susan Magrino's home on the top floor of a convert-ed carriage house has welcomed 150 people for a Christmas party and embraced twenty for a dinner buffet. Designed by her friend Alexis Stewart, the apartment is filled with 1940s-style furniture that gives it a tidy, ship-shape feeling. ABOVE Stuffy drapes were replaced with sleek wooden blinds. The coffee table is an original design by Heywood-Wake-field, a company that manufactured maple and birch furniture in the 1940s and 1950s. RIGHT Behind a Heywood-Wakefield record cabinet is a wall covered with porthole-like mirrors—a clever alternative to a mirrored wall.

An East Hampton cottage offers both community and privacy to the eight guests who share it during the summertime. The dining room, above, is the

physical and emotional center of the house. "It's jammed with people all summer long," says Stephen Earle, style director of MARTHA STEWART LIVING,

who bought and renovated the 1880s shingle-style house in 1994. Everyone collects around a 1920s dining table Earle found at a New York City auction;

with five leaves, it can expand to welcome August hordes as easily as it seats two or three during the off-season. The other rooms lead off the dining room

like spokes in a wheel, according to Earle. To the left is what is known as "the telephone room"; to the right is the living room. Both spaces are used for

intimate gatherings, but are too small to accommodate all the inhabitants at once. Yet the flow of the space is open and enticing; from any one room you

can see vistas into two or three others. Earle used color as a unifying element that also draws the eye from room to room: The beeswax color of the dining

room is picked up by a large pot in the telephone room, which is painted a shade of ocher; the living room is a paler version of that color.

During the renovation of the house, Earle extended the upstairs (left) to add a new master bedroom, bathroom, and storage room. Custom-made square windows line the new hallway, set low to let in light but also maintain privacy, since this side of the house faces the neighbors. The ocher color of the hall and stairway continues that of the front hall and living room (above); the painted floors help to unify the scheme. Earle customized standard store-bought paints by mixing in earth pigments to increase their complexity or adding white to lighten them.

ABOVE Rena and Paul Stallings thought a sprawling farmhouse kitchen would make a welcoming retreat for family and friends, so it was the first room they renovated after buying a dilapidated estate on Long Island's north shore. The 640-square-foot kitchen hadn't been modernized since 1927. Rather than gut it, they chose to spruce it up. The only major structural change: French doors replaced a window, flooding the room with light and giving access to the garden. The wooden table is used at all hours, for reading, working, and eating. It forms the heart of the room, which is itself the heart of the home. LEFT A butler's pantry lies halfway between the kitchen and dining room, like a gateway between intimate and formal.

LEFT Tin bread boxes left behind by the previous owner were stripped of their peeling paint and polished to a luminous sheen. They sit side by side with modern appliances beneath a cabinet full of Rena's kitchen collectibles, including enamelware, ironstone, and European hotel silver, acquired during buying trips for Henro, the antiques shop the Stallings own. Underneath each wooden countertop is an original built-in cutting board that can be pulled out for extra counter space. A combination of old and new fixtures, knobs, and hardware creates a feeling of relaxed authenticity. Some of the vintage pieces were found at flea markets, but quality reproductions often proved to be just as good. BELOW LEFT Window shelves were built above the old radiators; the brackets were copied from the supports for the kitchen cabinets. BELOW A two-hundred-square-foot butler's pantry was reorganized as a cleanup and storage room for dinnerware and glasses. It can be used to stockpile dishes without interfering with work going on in the kitchen or events in the dining room. Two new industrial-load dishwashers were installed; the cabinetry they ousted was moved to below the sink to conceal unsightly pipes.

OPPOSITE Gathering needn't involve a crowd. The library in Martha's East Hampton house is a quiet place where two good friends might sit and talk, or read in companionable silence. Windows face west, letting in warm afternoon light. Interior windows provide visual contact with the rest of the house while blocking out any distracting noises. The sofa is slipcovered in crisp, chintz-glazed linen. The slipcover on the armchair is made from a nineteenth-century linen damask tablecloth; the tea-dyed fringe was snipped from vintage tea towels. Touches of bright color enliven the neutral palette: garden roses in a mercury-glass vase, an antique tapestry pillow in crimson wool, an arrangement of dark-green McCoy vases. ABOVE In Alexis Stewart's redesigned carriage house, a Mission sofa is the only fixed piece. Everything else is lightweight and movable, as befits a small weekend space that serves many functions. Instead of creating artificial "rooms" out of furniture groupings, she has integrated the elements into a flexible, open plan. French doors allow a patio to become an extension of the living room; the wicker furniture and tile-topped tables are as at home in the sunshine as they are in this cool, stylish interior.

In East Hampton, Martha takes an inside-out approach to decorating for company, using garden furniture indoors during the off-season, and bringing traditional pieces outside in the summer. ABOVE A wicker chair mingles comfortably with more formal furniture; rattan garden chairs surround a marble-topped mahogany table. LEFT An armoire was painted with high-gloss enamel, then set on the porch and stocked with supplies for summer entertaining. OPPOSITE Come summer, people naturally congregate outdoors. To make them feel at home, Martha furnishes the porch like an interior room. Draperies made from awning fabric provide a sense of enclosure; the carpeting is coir, a natural fiber often used to cover diving boards.

OPPOSITE An old mirror hung on a hydrangea-covered wall brings a touch of sophisticated artifice to a garden's design. ABOVE In September, when the *Clematis paniculata* is in bloom, there's no sweeter place to spend time than in the shade of Martha's trellised pergola in East Hampton. A white chair and table are carried out from the house and set up alongside garden furniture for an impromptu tea. Pillows covered in all-weather fabric soften the hard edges of built-in benches. Martha designed this outdoor room to take advantage of its impressive view of the house, and she invites people to join her here only when, as she puts it, she has "something serious to say to them."

Windows

Four walls and a roof overhead don't make for much of a home if there aren't any windows to let in a bit of the world outside. But basic as they are to our sense of well-being, windows are far from simple—we ask more from them than from just about any other feature of our homes. Stanley Abercrombie outlines these expectations in *A Philosophy of Interior Design:* "To let in air but keep out rain, to allow view but maintain privacy, to let in light without cold (or excessively hot) air, dust, or noise, to let in air without light, and to vary at will the amounts of all these substances." Windows ought to look good while they're at it, too, and we've devised elaborate systems of fabrics, rods, weights, and pulleys to make sure they do.

The trick to successful window treatments is not to rely on prefabricated solutions, however, since the requirements you have of your windows won't be the same as anyone else's. Begin instead with the bare facts: What are the physical conditions and limitations of your windows, and how would you like to alter them? You may discover that you don't need to do anything at all. If you live in a house with lovely, private views and strong architectural window frames, there's no need to cover them up. An undressed window can make a dignified statement. But if you're like most people, you probably want a bit more control. A single system of draperies doesn't have to accomplish everything; sometimes layering treatments—a simple roller shade beneath a curtain, for example—creates a cleaner effect for less money. The first step is to consider the following variables.

APPEARANCE Since window treatments derive so much of their character from the pure flow of fabric itself, using quality materials is essential. Linen, cotton, silk, and wool are the best fibers, in weaves that are light and fluid

OPPOSITE Crown molding mounted inside a window frame becomes a cornice that hides the workings of a Roman shade attached to the inside with Velcro. The shade is made of glazed cotton, which lets in light while ensuring privacy. The cornice can be gilded to stand out as a design element or painted the same color as the window frame so that it disappears.

rather than heavy and drooping. Taffeta, damask, voile, and velvet are some traditional choices. Select colors that are a subtle play on the existing palette of the room; beautiful curtains often derive their impact from texture and shape rather than bright, noisy patterns.

Because of their inherent drama, window treatments can easily overwhelm a room, and should be considered a finishing touch rather than a starting point in any interior. "A window treatment should be in balance with the rest of the furnishings," says Ann Baderian Polokoff, a designer and upholstery consultant in New York City. "If you haven't finished decorating yet, you don't know how much window treatment you need." She recommends starting out with something simple, like Venetian blinds or white roller shades, that can become the underpinning of a more elaborate treatment later on.

CARE AND DURABILITY You may love wide-open windows, but your curtains will pay for it, especially if you live in an urban environment. Cotton or linen can be washed if the curtains are simply constructed and the fabric is untreated (the glazing on chintzes, for example, will wash away, ruining the fabric). Dirt actually destroys certain fabrics, such as silk, if it's allowed to settle into the fibers; window treatments should be vacuumed regularly. Fabrics such as linen wrinkle easily and are best used for designs that won't be opened and closed often. In general, natural fibers are sturdier and longer lasting than synthetics.

VIEW A great view is like a work of art, and shouldn't be covered up. Choose shades and blinds that roll or fold up tightly and disappear at the top of the frame. If you hang curtains, extend the rod beyond the edges of the window frame, so that the fabric can be pushed aside. But what if only half your view is worth gazing at? You can enjoy the sky and treetops but block out the neighbor's backyard with café curtains hung from the middle of the frame down to the sill, or with shades that pull up from the bottom rather than down from the top.

LIGHT Precious as sunlight is during the dark days of winter, it has a harmful side too, damaging art, wood, and fabrics. Nor is it always illuminating; too much of it is as hard to see by as too little. Fine, thin weaves such as voile or muslin give sunlight a translucent, milky quality. For more precise control, consider venetian blinds, which can be adjusted as the light changes throughout the day. If the sun is still too strong, consider optic blinds, made from a synthetic fabric that lets in light and views without glare or heat. Finally, if you want to be able to shut out light entirely, line heavy drapes or shades with dense, tightly woven fabrics.

NOISE AND TEMPERATURE The same layers that muffle noise also block drafts. In summer, when massive draperies look inappropriate, lined curtains of linen, silk, or cotton offer some padding against a cacophony outdoors.

ARCHITECTURE Curtains, shades, and blinds can articulate the strong lines of a well-made window or disguise the shape of a poor one. An elegant column is created by window treatments that drop from ceiling to floor. They can follow the edge of an equally tall window, or begin at a rod mounted six inches or more above the cornice to elongate a squat window. Translucent shades that fill the frame reflect the panes behind them in a soft grid. Wooden blinds, with their strong horizontal lines, create an architectural pattern all their own.

One final consideration that Polokoff brings to bear on the selection of window treatments is how they look from the outside. A neat facade can be spoiled by mismatched curtains and blinds. You will probably have concerns of your own (cats that may be tempted to climb curtains, for example). Consider utility first, invest in quality materials, and beauty will follow of its own accord.

Tailored Roman shades with horizontal wooden battens play against the verticality of tall, narrow windows. Mounted at three-quarters height, they let in sunlight while affording privacy. The clean lines of the shades echo the forties style of the armchair by Donghia; the cotton taffeta fabric provides a touch of formality.

OPPOSITE A pale fabric laminated to roller-shade backing becomes a translucent screen in a sunny bedroom. To block light, a blackout backing could be layered between the fabric and the shade. Reverse-roll brackets hide the rolls neatly behind the shades. Inexpensive roller shades (bottom), available at hardware stores, are the simplest way to cover windows. They can be dressed up with customized pulls, like the Bakelite rings and raffia dressmaker's frogs shown here (see also page 60); tassels, large beads, or wooden rings can also be used. ABOVE A casual blue canvas roll-up shade is rigged with nautical hardware and thick cotton cording. The exposed mechanism becomes part of the design; the sailor's cleat used as an anchor (see detail on page 60) completes the breezy, nautical effect. The floppy ends of the striped shade (right) are created by sewing ring tabs eight inches in from the sides rather than at the edges. This design— a variation on a Roman shade called a butterfly shade—is best used on a window that is at least three feet wide; its graceful curves would be lost in a narrower space. To fill the window, two lengths of fabric were sewn together horizontally; the seam is hidden inside fabric folds.

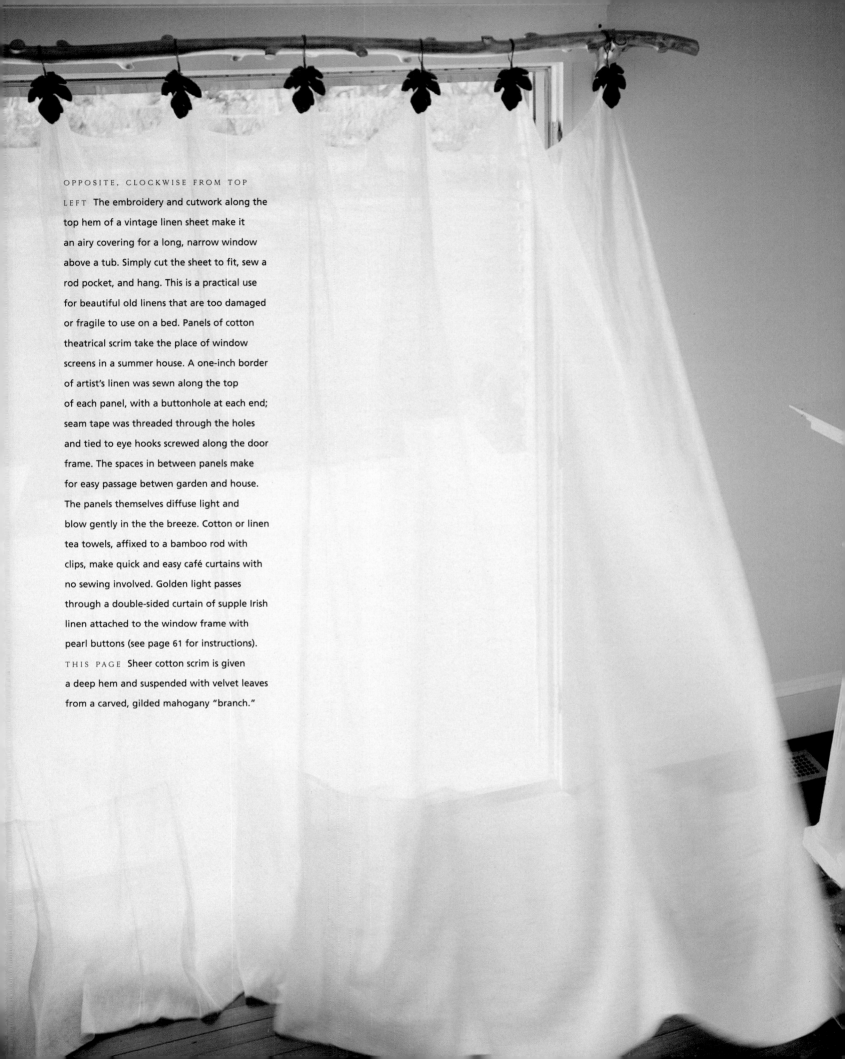

OPPOSITE, CLOCKWISE FROM TOP
LEFT The embroidery and cutwork along the
top hem of a vintage linen sheet make it
an airy covering for a long, narrow window
above a tub. Simply cut the sheet to fit, sew a
rod pocket, and hang. This is a practical use
for beautiful old linens that are too damaged
or fragile to use on a bed. Panels of cotton
theatrical scrim take the place of window
screens in a summer house. A one-inch border
of artist's linen was sewn along the top
of each panel, with a buttonhole at each end;
seam tape was threaded through the holes
and tied to eye hooks screwed along the door
frame. The spaces in between panels make
for easy passage betwen garden and house.
The panels themselves diffuse light and
blow gently in the the breeze. Cotton or linen
tea towels, affixed to a bamboo rod with
clips, make quick and easy café curtains with
no sewing involved. Golden light passes
through a double-sided curtain of supple Irish
linen attached to the window frame with
pearl buttons (see page 61 for instructions).
THIS PAGE Sheer cotton scrim is given
a deep hem and suspended with velvet leaves
from a carved, gilded mahogany "branch."

ABOVE LEFT Wooden cornice boards were traditional in colonial American houses, where their curves were intended to emulate the drape of more expensive fabrics. The pattern for this one was adopted from cornices in Martha Stewart's Westport house. It hides the mechanism of the painted wood blinds and lends presence to a plain frame. ABOVE RIGHT Wooden-slat blinds bring an informal, outdoor look inside. These have a valance, or decorative flap, at the top, which is folded to the back for a cleaner effect. RIGHT Woven vinyl mesh, an industrial material, makes a subtly beautiful and practical shade. It resists deterioration from the sun and filters out heat as well as light.

In choosing window treatments, it's important to keep in mind not only aesthetic considerations but practical ones as well; you should be able to tailor a treatment to suit your needs as well as your taste. Sheer on top and heavier below, this linen Roman shade is perfect for a city bedroom, granting privacy and light as the same time. The rings attached to the reverse side, which control the shade's folds, are usually sewn to a tape that is then sewn to the back of the shade. With a fabric as sheer as this one, the rings must be sewn directly to the back of the shade. Tiny horizontal tucks were sewn into the fabric to give the rings a sturdier place to grip.

SHADES AND BLINDS

Shades and blinds are the most forthright of window treatments. Contemporary as they look, they are also among the oldest. Shades are soft window coverings, usually made of fabric, that can be raised and lowered. There are two types: roller shades, which wind up smoothly around a narrow cylinder, and those controlled by a system of cords and pulleys, the simplest of which are Roman shades. Blinds are hard, slatted window coverings that run horizontally or vertically and can be drawn by contracting, rolling, or folding. The hardware required to operate shades and blinds is quite simple, but it can provide an opportunity for small decorative touches. 1 An upside-down stainless-steel hook makes a simple shade anchor (this one fastens the Roman shades on page 53). It's attached to the front of the window frame, but families with small children should place shade hooks out of reach. 2 A side view of the same shade shows how pleats are formed. Rings sewn to the seam behind each dowel are threaded with cord; when the cord is pulled, rings and dowels stack up. 3 Roller shades like the ones shown on page 54 can be customized with decorative hardware. We've attached Bakelite rings and braided raffia dressmaker's frogs using epoxy glue. 4 A chrome-plated brass nautical cleat secures the cord of the canvas roll-up shade shown on page 55. 5 The cording runs through pulleys, which hang from cup hooks. The shade itself is suspended on a tension rod. 6 Venetian-blind slats and cotton-blend twill tapes can be ordered in custom hues. (See the wooden venetian blinds with contrasting tapes on page 58.) 7 A vintage porcelain picture nail secures the Roman shade shown on page 59. The natural-twine shade cord is finished with real bone beads.

HOW TO MAKE A BUTTON CURTAIN; CURTAIN RINGS

To make a button-edged curtain like the one shown above and on page 56, cut two pieces of contrasting fabric (and lining if the fabrics are sheer) 1¾" wider and longer than your window. With right sides facing, stitch pieces together ¼" in from edges along three sides, leaving the bottom free. Turn right sides out, press, and hem. Make 1" buttonholes about 6" apart along the top edge and one hole on the right side of the curtain at the hem. Stitch fuzzy side of 1"-wide Velcro tape to a same-width length of grosgrain ribbon, face out. Sew ¾" pearl buttons to the ribbon through the Velcro so that buttons align with buttonholes. Mount the stiff side of the Velcro tape along the top of the window frame using non-water-soluble glue. Attach its fuzzy mate with buttons facing out. Button curtain onto window frame. Make a tieback by hammering a flat-topped nail into the left side of the

window frame and gluing a button to the nail. Lift up the right corner of the curtain and button it to the tieback. This button-on curtain can easily be reversed or removed for cleaning.

It's possible to make a functional window treatment using unexpected devices, such as the buttons and Velcro above. But traditional curtain hardware is often beautiful in its own right, and can double as decoration while serving its appointed function. The metal curtain rings shown above, top right, are shaped like leaves, arrows, and tendrils. They can be tied or sewn to fabric. All are brass except the large leaf, which is iron; the leaf on the far right is antique, the rest new. Above right are more rings, some with eyelets onto which curtains can be sewn or hooked. From left: a brass fleur-de-lis; gilded mahogany; the same, but more simply shaped; painted, with band beading.

A comfortable bedroom is equally restful to body, mind, and soul. Extraneous clutter has been banished to other areas of this vast loft. A cotton canopy and scrim curtains are hung around a contemporary tiger-maple teaser bed to muffle noise and create a sense of intimacy and enclosure. A pure and simple bathroom, opposite, meets the requirements of its owner with quiet dignity. Alexis Stewart, Martha's daughter, used inexpensive ceramic subway tiles for the walls and hexagonal tiles for the floor so she could splurge on things like the Speakman polished-chrome fittings in the tub. Pristine as this bathroom is, it's not devoid of life; a narrow shelf above the tub allows Alexis to display a vibrant collection of nineteenth-century green opaline glass.

Comfort

It's the ultimate indulgence, but you don't need a fortune to create it

OPPOSITE "I do everything in the bedroom," says Martha Stewart. "I read, watch TV, I have my computer there. It's my refuge." A floor-to-ceiling screen blocks off the work area from the rest of the rooms; it's made of panels of green milk glass and white linen fitted into a frame adapted from a kit for exterior shutters. The windows are curtainless, since Martha likes to wake up with the sun. Coats of glossy white paint unify a variety of furniture styles. Martha had her Victorian oak bed lengthened by three inches; she sleeps on a horsehair mattress covered with silk batting, between vintage linen sheets embroidered with her initial (above). Two large bedside tables are actually café tables with cast-iron bases that Martha had topped in galvanized steel; they hold piles of books, and writing material in case she's seized by inspiration in the middle of the night. The linen rug on the floor is gentle on the feet; "It's nice to get out on," she says.

BETWEEN TOO HARD AND TOO SOFT, TOO HOT AND TOO COLD, TOO big and too small, lies comfort—and it feels just right. But though, like Goldilocks, we know it when we find it, comfort is difficult to define. "In practice, it is much easier to measure discomfort than comfort," writes Witold Rybczynski in *Home: A Short History of an Idea.* "Comfort is both something simple and complicated. It incorporates many transparent layers of meaning— privacy, ease, convenience—some of which are buried deeper than others."

Comfort should inspire every decorating scheme, but its special province is intimate spaces: the bedrooms and bathrooms tucked away in the recesses of a home. Here, personal whims and indulgences can be given free rein. Yet apart from buying matching linens, many people hardly decorate these private rooms at all. They equip them adequately for the most basic pursuits—sleeping, bathing, getting dressed—while ignoring the much more complex scenes played out here every day. The truth is, people eat, drink, read, write, talk on the phone, watch television, exercise, and groom every inch of their bodies in their bedrooms and bathrooms. And if these activities aren't planned for, they wind up being accommodated in an ad hoc fashion. The result is a bedside table overflowing with books and boxes of tissues, and a hair dryer that lies sinkside until it gets stuffed into a cabinet on cleaning day.

Clutter is not comfortable. Ease, calm, and beauty are. To make bedrooms and baths true places of refuge, take an inventory of the activities that go on there, then design ways to handle each one. If your sink is a jumble of bottles and jars, bring an enamel-topped table into the bathroom to use as a vanity. Set up chairs and a table at the foot of a bed for reading, eating, or getting dressed. Use a desk or refectory table at bedside. Provide racks for every towel and lamps for every task. Use antique mirrors and rugs in unexpected places. Make every activity effortless—and beautiful.

Common sense has an important role to play in designing comforting spaces. Twelve pillows at the head of a bed and a bathtub big enough for a sumo wrestler aren't so much comfortable as ostentatious. If the tub takes hours to fill and the pillows have to be moved aside each night, they don't really suit their users anyway and will soon become downright annoying. The best way to avoid such mistakes is to be guided by all the senses when decorating these spaces. Anything beyond what is soft and easy against the skin, bright and inviting to the eyes, warm to bare feet, quiet to the ears, and clean and fresh to the nose is too much. For comfort is like a cradle poised between extremes. When all the simplest human needs are met with gentle grace, comfort becomes the greatest luxury of all.

When Martha designed her East Hampton bathroom, she first considered exactly how she wanted to use it, then acquired the fixtures and accessories to make it work. Rather than installing a combined shower-bath, she included a claw-footed tub for relaxing soaks and a separate glass stall for more efficient showers. Both are big enough to permit a full range of motion: In the shower there's plenty of room to bend over to retrieve a fallen bar of soap or to step out of the water's path; the tub is long and deep enough for a full-body stretch. Fittings were mounted in the wall so the tub could fit snugly in the corner by the window. Martha found the cupboard hung high above the tub in a bedroom of the house when she moved in. A white-painted button chair is pulled up to the zinc-topped pastry table used as a bathroom vanity (above). On its broad surface, a wide range of toiletries stays neat and accessible.

THIS PAGE AND OPPOSITE **A guest**
bathroom is outfitted to anticipate the needs
of visitors, with plenty of plush towels and
extras of any supplies they may have forgot-
ten. An ivory hairbrush and hand mirror rest
on a Gothic Revival pew chair. By the sink,
wood-scented soaps and a toothbrush are
placed in nineteenth-century horn dishes. The
ebonized mirror over the sink was originally
designed to hold hats in a foyer; the pegs now
proffer linen hand towels. Functional as this
room is, it's hardly clinical. Martha brings it to
life with unexpected elements such as the
Gothic-style cast-iron mirror by the window
and the hooked rug from Nova Scotia. A pair
of tramp-art pedestals supports the mirror and
a vase of rose hips from Martha's garden without using up much of the limited floor space.

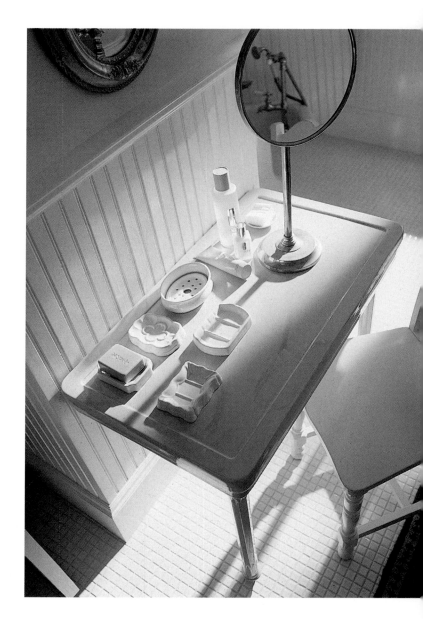

OPPOSITE, CLOCKWISE FROM TOP LEFT Martha found these mint-condition Victorian green-glass accessories at an architectural-salvage store. On a sleek celadon porcelain bathroom table from the 1880s, Martha has arranged a collection of ironstone soap dishes and an antique shaving mirror she found in Portland, Oregon. A reproduction porcelain-and-antiqued-brass knob feels reassuringly sturdy in the hand. Photographer Anita Calero found the nickel sink for her weekend house in Texas; it was taken from an old yacht. She slips fragrant soaps between her towels to scent them. ABOVE A tub in one of Martha's guest bathrooms is set into a slab of the same Carrera marble that's used to cover the walls. Cut to fit neatly around the rim, the cool, chalky marble forms a lip that keeps water from splashing out. ABOVE RIGHT A chrome double towel bar by Czech & Speake holds Martha's monogrammed hand towels. RIGHT To ensure that the third-floor bathroom in her East Hampton house remains well stocked with towels, Martha turned a doctor's cabinet that she found in a junk shop in Portland into a linen chest. Originally bright pink, the cabinet was refinished in white enamel.

With a little planning, even a small bathroom can satisfy basic requirements and still keep chaos under control. A tapered apple-picking ladder, left, creates an extra towel rack in a beach house that's overrun with visitors all summer long. When Stephen Earle renovated the small bathroom below, he realized there wouldn't be room enough for a table or freestanding cabinet, so he selected a sink with extra-wide edges. Now there's plenty of surface space to set toiletries on. A shelf above the toilet holds cotton balls and swabs, and the wainscoting and medicine cabinet are topped by wide ledges that provide extra shelving as well. After seeing high-priced vintage medicine cabinets in antiques shops, Earle decided to make one himself. He embellished a mirrored door found in a junkyard with old hardware and hung it on a box made from wood molding and stripping. OPPOSITE Cloaked in a thick cotton-terry slipcover, a vintage wooden folding chair becomes an inviting place for manicuring or for blow-drying hair.

LEFT AND OPPOSITE Martha gave in to flights of fancy when planning the first-floor bathrooms in her Westport and East Hampton houses. Both rooms are quite limited in size and scope, but manage to convey an airy atmosphere nonetheless. The Westport bathroom (left) contains a contemporary version of an antique French pedestal washstand that Martha fell in love with twenty-three years ago when she spied it through a shop window. She added the fittings, made of porcelain and antiqued brass (see detail on page 70). A polished mahogany side table enhances the room's feeling of elegance, as do the French bronze doré swing-arm sconces on either side of the gilded mirror. The East Hampton bathroom (opposite) includes touches of pure charm, such as a Corinthian-columned medicine cabinet that was handcrafted in Newport, Rhode Island, around 1915, and an ironstone vase filled with yellow-and-white pheasant's eye narcissus from the garden. Spindly nickel legs lend a delicate feeling to the old marble sink, and the stone surface itself has acquired the soft golden-brown patina of age.

OPPOSITE An East Hampton guest bathroom is well equipped but not over-crowded; there are plenty of empty surfaces where toiletries and clothes can be laid out. A limited palette and choice of materials keeps the mood restful. The floor is covered in turquoise-dyed cement tiles from Mexico; the color is repeated in the shower curtain of striped cotton duck, the whimsical Victorian mirror above the reproduction sink, and the cast-iron mirror by the tub. An enamel-topped 1930s kitchen table with its legs chopped off serves as a place to stack towels. ABOVE RIGHT An assortment of delicious bedding materials turns a mahogany sleigh bed into a sumptuous place to sleep late. Embroidered cotton sheets are topped by a blanket of cashmere and merino wool and a down com-forter covered in silk charmeuse. RIGHT In a quiet garret room, a simple bed is dressed with luxurious minimalism. Flannel sheets are covered with a square of raspberry cashmere edged with blanket stitching (see page 80 for instructions).

OPPOSITE A space comes to life at the foot of a bed to gracefully handle the overflow of activities that go on in this dormered room. A farm table capped with galvanized steel is the perfect place for a breakfast tray, and a pair of vintage Lloyd's loom chairs welcomes private talks. A reproduction Fulper lamp sits on a rattan sofa table. The pillows and bed are covered in sturdy antique ticking. ABOVE Carefully selected furniture makes the most of limited space in a guest bedroom. Voluminous chests of drawers double as bedside tables. Atop them is a pair of bedside lamps made from nineteenth-century English seltzer bottles; towels and books are close at hand. The chests are turn-of-the-century faux bamboo; the bed and picture frames are made from the real thing. The walls are painted a serene neutral; the ceiling an ethereal blue.

ABOVE AND OPPOSITE Comfort often has a nostalgic side. Two simple rooms in Martha's East Hampton house evoke memories of being tucked into childhood beds. The mismatched brass beds above are nineteenth-century American. White matelassé coverlets are spread smooth beneath home-woven striped wool blankets from the 1930s. A pottery lamp acquired from a flea market lends a bright note to the room, and repeats the color of the house's exterior trim just visible at the edge of the window. A beaded-board ceiling painted robin's-egg blue is a soothing sight to wake up to. Three pristine beds (opposite) are lined up in an attic room, awaiting visits from Martha's nieces. The summer-weight cotton chenille coverlets are from the 1950s, and recall the innocent pleasure of nodding off in a bedroom devoted to nothing but sleep.

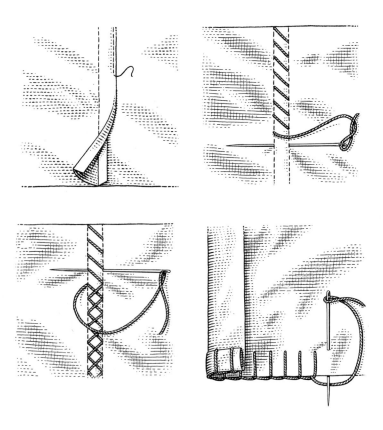

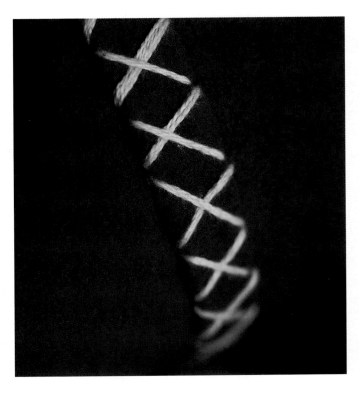

HOW TO MAKE A DECORATIVELY STITCHED BLANKET

Start with a piece of fabric 3" longer and wider than finished blanket dimensions. The queen-size (90"-by-90") square of raspberry cashmere on page 75 has a seam down the middle, providing a place for a decorative cross-stitch (above right). If you choose to do the same, join two fabric lengths with a flat-felled seam; cross-stitch over the seam. Edge the blanket with a blanket stitch: Turn and lightly press all edges under ¾", then ¾" again, overlapping corners. Pin or baste in place. Work the stitches so that they encase the ¾" folded hem and are spaced ½" apart. At each corner, make one stitch on a diagonal. Instructions for these three simple sewing methods follow (see diagrams above).
1 FLAT-FELLED SEAM Lay one piece of fabric atop the other, and pin along one length. Machine-stitch 1½" in from edge. Press seam open, then to one side. Trim concealed seam allowance to ½". Press under edge of top seam allowance ⅜". Position it evenly over the trimmed edge; pin in place. Machine-stitch the folded edge to the blanket ⅛" in from edge, parallel to previous seam. Press flat. 2 CROSS-STITCH Using a tapestry needle and worsted-weight cotton yarn, cross-stitch over the seam. Hold the blanket right side up, seam facing you. At the far end, pull the needle through from wrong side to right, emerging on the left side of the seam at the edge. Insert needle diagonally down through the right line of stitching and out horizontally through the left. Make a second diagonal stitch parallel to the first, with space between stitches equal to the width of the seam. Continue stitching to create an entire row of diagonal floats across the seam. When you reach the end, reverse direction. 3 Work the same stitch heading away from you, still moving from right to left. The new floats will cross the old, forming a series of X's. 4 BLANKET STITCH Use the same needle and yarn to edge the blanket. Hold one edge toward you with the right side up. Starting at the left-hand corner, draw the yarn out through fold from inside the hem. Insert needle down into fabric, ½" to the right and ¾" in from edge. Bring it out at the edge, as shown, keeping yarn loop under needle. Continue stitching, working left to right, until all sides are edged.

HOW TO MAKE A BED

Martha Stewart has her own easy, efficient system for making a bed. Begin with a good-quality mattress and box spring. 1 Protect the mattress with a cotton cover; Martha adds a wool pad. 2 Flat sheets are preferable to fitted ones, because they don't pull or tear. Make hospital corners, starting at the bed's head: After draping the sheet evenly over the bed about one foot beyond the head, stand toward the center and pick up a side hem. Pull hem toward you into a taut crease, then raise the creased section over the mattress. With the other hand, smooth sheet flat along mattress's side. Fold the creased section down over the side, removing one hand as you tuck the sheet under the mattress with the other. Repeat at foot and other side of bed. 3 Add top sheet; make hospital corners at the foot. 4 Leave sides untucked for easier sleeping. Finish with a coverlet or comforter.

A SIMPLE DUST RUFFLE

It's hard to decide which is the bigger eyesore: an exposed box spring or some of the froufrou dust ruffles currently on the market. One easy, low-cost solution is to cover the box spring with a drape of rectangular fabric. A tablecloth, bedsheet, or any interesting piece of cloth will do the job nicely. Even better, this simple dust ruffle will be a cinch to wash and iron. If you use a sheet, choose one that is the same size as the bed: a single for a single bed, a queen for a queen. For a tablecloth or length of fabric, first try it out on the box spring—with luck, it will be a perfect fit. If it's not, determine the correct width by doubling the height of the box spring and adding its width plus six inches. This creates a rectangle of fabric that covers the box spring and hangs down an extra two inches all the way around, after you've sewn a one-inch hem.

Light

Light does more than banish darkness. It can bathe a room in a soft glow, sparkle across a table set with crystal and silver, and bounce off polished wood floors, picking up color and texture all the way. Light displays energy and motion even when it seems

to be perfectly still. And it attracts the eye and the body—for like moths, we are drawn to its warmth.

Decorating with light isn't simply a matter of illuminating a space. Although it's important to keep people from bumping into things, overlighting can also be a problem. When the sun goes down, most of us are inclined to replace it with a great glowing orb stuck smack in the middle of a ceiling. Such brightness isn't necessary—after all, the human eye can take in even the thinnest veil of light in a moonlit garden—nor is it particularly beautiful. "People have a light-it-up attitude," says Stephen Earle, MARTHA STEWART LIVING'S style direc-

tor. "It loses one of the most romantic qualities of decorating. Lighting isn't just about lamps. It's a whole level of a space that needs to be considered." Before learning to decorate with light, it's necessary to understand its many roles. There are three basic kinds of lighting: ambient, task, and decorative. A combination of all three makes for the most useful and satisfying rooms.

AMBIENT LIGHTING Also called general light, ambient light is the light that suffuses a room with an even glow, filling in shadows and softening the transition between bright and dark. Ambient light is essential for general vision and a sense of ease and comfort in a room (imagine, by comparison, the unsettling mood of a room lit by spotlights—pools of glare surrounded by blackness). But used by itself, ambient light is as bland as a cloudy day.

TASK LIGHTING As its name suggests, this is focused light that illuminates particular areas of activity. Task lighting

OPPOSITE Three different light sources give texture and depth to Martha Stewart's East Hampton living room. Glass and polished mahogany surfaces multiply the effects. A standing lamp illuminates an American Empire card table. An alabaster lamp glows on a Greek Revival display cabinet; strip lighting behind the pediment lights a collection of neoclassical metal urns.

is needed for reading, writing, sewing, cooking, and grooming, among other things. But task lighting can't do its job alone: While a work surface should be bright, it shouldn't be too much brighter than surrounding areas, since high contrast will strain the eyes. Lamps used for task lighting should also be at eye level, so that the glaring bulb within is never visible beneath the shade.

DECORATIVE LIGHTING Less utilitarian than the other two types, decorative lighting takes advantage of light's dramatic powers to draw the eye. It can call attention to something other than itself, such as a spotlit painting or an urn. Or it can be a delightful sight in and of itself.

Most lighting fixtures play a combination of these roles. A typical table lamp, for example, emits a pool of bright task light downward and radiates ambient light upward through the top of its shade. Yet just because a single lamp can perform many functions doesn't mean you should rely on just one or two fixtures to address all your lighting needs. Several small lamps give more character to a room than one or two big fixtures used on their own.

DESIGNING WITH LIGHT Composing a lighting scheme should be approached the same way as arranging other elements of an interior: with an eye to utility, color, and balance. The first step is to address basic needs. Place task lighting where it's required; these bright points of light will form the underlying structure to an overall plan. Then add ambient light to fill in the dark spots and decorative light for character and depth.

Vary the brightness of lamps and lighting fixtures. This not only affects the level of illumination, it also dapples a room in color, since lower-watt bulbs have a yellower cast than white, high-watt bulbs. In general, halogen bulbs emit whiter, sharper light than incandescent bulbs. It's easy to experiment with brightness. When Stephen Earle finished decorating his East Hampton house, he bought a dozen

bulbs in a range of wattages, from fifteen to 150. He then tried out various combinations of bulbs in his lamps until he was satisfied with the overall effect in each room.

Lampshades add another layer of interest to a lighting scheme. Translucent shades of linen, rice paper, or parchment give a soft, milky quality to light. A colored silk shade will tint the light passing through it and shed a stain on nearby surfaces. Even an opaque shade can alter the color of light; the interior can be gilded or lined with colored fabric or paper.

LIVING WITH LIGHT Since most rooms host a variety of activities, a lighting scheme should be as versatile as possible. When entertaining friends, for example, the lamp used to illuminate work at the dining table should be dimmed to a hush.

Improving the versatility of a lighting scheme doesn't require a big investment. When Eric Pike, art director of MARTHA STEWART LIVING, moved into his home, he immediately replaced all his wall switches with dimmers. The impact was astonishing: Where once there was a single note of brightness, he created a range of tones from a warm glow to a cheerful shine. A table or standing lamp wired to take a three-way bulb will also acquire a new range of possibilities. And a lamp that has two sockets should be fitted with bulbs of different intensities—one forty and the other one hundred watts, for example—so it can serve various functions.

Finally, never underestimate the power of firelight and daylight. They are what our eyes are adapted for, and they have tremendous psychological powers. A sun-filled window is not only a tremendous boon for readers or menders, it's also a mood lifter, as recent studies have shown. And a few candles in unexpected places—a kitchen or bathroom, for example—can bring a kind of living mystery to an otherwise functional space.

A multipurpose lighting scheme suits this open-plan room used for both work and entertaining. A bamboo floor lamp designed by Isamu Noguchi is topped by a rice-paper shade to radiate soft ambient light into the air around it. On the French farmhouse table that serves as a desk, a bronze Art Nouveau lamp is fitted with a three-way bulb so it can be brightened for working evenings, dimmed for a more intimate mood. A black metal lamp from the 1950s provides task light for reading on a wicker chair; holes pierced in the shade create pinpoints of light. On a coffee table made of a sheet of three-quarter-inch plate glass propped on four terra-cotta pipe sections, a cluster of beeswax candles provides a mesmerizing flicker.

There's no need to overlight a hallway; a twenty-five-watt bulb every ten feet provides enough illumination to get around easily and makes arriving at a brightly lit destination all the more satisfying. At the end of the hall, a mercury-glass table lamp fitted with a seventy-five-watt bulb sits on a marble-topped side table. Overhead bulbs are covered with simple eight-inch clip-on paper lampshades; screw-in extensions from a hardware store were used to lower the bulbs, allowing light to spill out over the shades onto the ceiling. OPPOSITE Lampshades lend color and shape to light. An overhead fixture designed for factory use in the 1920s, top left, sheds a parabola of light downward; the corrugated, silvered surface inside intensifies light. In the bathroom beyond, a ceramic-based lamp sits on a sinkside table, a comforting touch in a utilitarian room. A mercury-glass-urn lamp base, top right, supports a shade covered in khaki silk and lined with pale blue to cool the color of incandescent light. The plush surface of a velvet shade, bottom right, absorbs light, so it always looks soft and shadowy. A drum-shaped fabric shade, bottom left, looks chic with black satin ribbon glued over the shade's metal struts.

ABOVE A matte tubular picture lamp all but disappears against a rustic bookshelf, but it's an important decorative asset nonetheless, lending definition

to the facade. Books are interspersed with decorative objects rather than being packed solidly onto the shelves. A diminutive night-light, above right,

is all that's needed to see your way to the bathroom at night. This one was made by removing the plastic shade from a hardware-store night-light, then

creating a new shade by twisting together leaves from Victorian beaded flowers. OPPOSITE TOP Cantilevered lamps, originally designed for offices,

are useful at bedside as well. One of a contemporary Italian pair is turned toward the wall, creating ambient light; the other is pulled close for reading.

OPPOSITE BOTTOM A modern aluminum sconce washes a wall in ambient light. When selecting lighting fixtures, it isn't necessary to take period styles

too literally—electric light hasn't been around as long as most antiques anyway. A well-proportioned, elegant fixture can seem at home in almost any room.

OPPOSITE "It's very ultra ultra," says Martha of the 1920s Venetian chandelier she found at a consignment shop. It could easily play several roles, providing task light to dine by, ambient light to soften the surrounding darkness, and making a decorative statement as well. But a chandelier should never be used alone—when the bulbs are bright enough to illuminate the room, looking at the fixture becomes uncomfortable. Instead, other light sources come into play: a cut-glass lamp from the 1930s, candles on the table and mantel. THIS PAGE In a guest room, overhead bed lamps were made by hanging gooseneck sconces upside down and replacing the glass shades with pleated, fringed silk.

Equipment made to withstand the commotion of a professional laboratory is a sensible choice for a hard-working kitchen. Alexis Stewart, who designed it, ordered these easy-to-clean, corrosion-resistant cabinets from Duralab, a Brooklyn-based company. OPPOSITE In a mudroom off her East Hampton kitchen, Martha Stewart can stay connected to her magazine offices. A 1940s desk chair pulls up to a farm table topped with galvanized aluminum. A vintage pie cabinet is bolted to the wall for overhead storage. Panels of homosote covered in linen turn the wall into a memo board.

Working

How to create stylish, functional spaces that work as hard as you do

ABOVE With refurbished used office equipment, a home office can be designed on a shoestring. A pair of file cabinets in Martha's East Hampton office was taken to an auto-body shop to be spray-painted Araucana Porcelain Green; it now has a sleek, lacquered finish. File boxes were made from the same galvanized aluminum that tops the desk.

OPPOSITE Classic white subway tile used for the backsplash in Alexis's kitchen takes the clinical edge off the room's design. The front of the sink is vented to keep trapped fumes from building up in a lab. The countertop is easy to clean; Duralab surfaces are welded rather than screwed together, so there are no crevices to collect dirt.

FOR YEARS, THE HOME HAS BEEN CONSIDERED A PLACE OF LEISURE, the nest you return to after work. But that idea is more myth than reality. The average home has always been as busy a hive of productivity as any office building. The care and maintenance of a house and its inhabitants—the cooking, cleaning, gardening, repairs, paperwork, and creative arts required for their upkeep—have long been women's full-time careers.

Still, in the past decade, the line between the workplace and the home has blurred. Forty-three million Americans now do paid work from home at least part-time, and the number is rising. The type of work has changed too, since computers and faxes have made it possible to be electronically connected to an office hundreds of miles away.

Someday soon, a home office may be featured in the blueprint for every new house. In the meantime, incorporating high-tech equipment into the plan and decor of an existing home can take a bit of effort. It's one thing to hide a television set inside an armoire; it's another to fit an entire office in there. Instead of trying to disguise a work space, aim to make it efficient, orderly, and comfortable. The result should be crisp and classic enough to blend in with any decor. After all, utility has never been incompatible with beauty, as Martha Stewart knows. For years, she has been furnishing her homes with equipment made for doctors' offices, laboratories, and factories.

Furniture designed for professional spaces really is the most practical choice for home offices and workshops. Working at a desk that's the right elevation in a chair with lower-back support is not merely self-indulgent, it's also healthy and smart. And a kitchen outfitted with restaurant or laboratory equipment adjusted to your height and reach will enable you to cook for hours without damaging your neck, back, or legs. It's also wise to look to artists' and writers' studios for ideas when designing a home workplace. Even

if your creations aren't quite on a par with those of Henri Matisse or Irving Penn, your workplace should feel vital and inspiring. Don't just thumbtack vacation photos to the bulletin board and consider it done; fill the room with furniture and accessories that please and stimulate your senses. Spending a day working at home should never seem like punishment, nor should it quarantine you from the people who delight you. Set aside a corner for coffee breaks; arrange a table with coloring books or computer games for the children; make sure there's lots of light. And don't feel guilty if your finished space features a daybed or easy chair. A moment's quiet repose will allow you to return to your computer or casserole filled with the fresh ideas and energy that are the keys to real success.

Duralab components look classic enough to blend with most decorating schemes, whether ordered as freestanding units or continuous cabinetry. Alexis used both to outfit her kitchen. The storage case, right, has glass-front doors, so contents are easy to identify. Duralab metal is interlined with cardboard sound baffling, so cabinet doors are quiet and stable rather than clanky. Vintage mason jars and new surgical beakers hold staples within. A stainless-steel medical-instrument cart beside the cabinet allows Alexis to roll a television to any convenient spot. In the laundry room, below, Duralab components in Pearl finish look as bright as bleached cotton. A lab table provides a sanitary surface for folding clean clothes; the undershelf keeps bulky baskets out of the way. A hanging cabinet hides detergent and bleach.

LEFT Photographer Jan Staller used Duralab equipment in Eye-rest Green t[...] his New York City loft. Cooking equipment and collectibles are stored in glass-front cabinets that divide the kitchen from the living room. BELOW LEFT A lab table with a stainless-steel top provides a surface for eating or working in Alexis's kitchen; aluminum office chairs are tucked beneath. BELOW Alexis determined the exact configuration of deep and shallow drawers she needed to store food and utensils. Inside a low cabinet, a pull-out shelf gives easy access to short jars and cans; taller bottles fit easily underneath.

OPPOSITE For his home office, Jan Staller had a flat-file manufacturer match the Eye-rest Green of his built-in Duralab desk. A red Harry Bertoia chair provides vivid contrast. Red-oak floors are bleached and stained gray for a cool, workmanlike look. The glass-front cabinet to the left is on casters, so it acts as both a movable wall and curiosity case. THIS PAGE A single Duralab cabinet becomes a rolling tool chest in a garage that doubles as a workshop. Different drawer depths accommodate screws and drill bits as well as large tools and cables.

Rather than sacrifice an entire room of her Westport house to an office, Martha designed a compact work space that can disappear behind closed doors. She tore down a wall of outdated cupboards and designed a new system of four closets. The one at right houses computer and printer, fax machine, TV monitor, stereo, and phone. Sliding trays, above, give access to whatever equipment she needs at the moment. A homosote board turns the inside of the door into a memo board. OPPO-SITE Professional kitchens inspired the proportions but not the materials of Martha's East Hampton kitchen. Counters are thirty-eight inches high, so she doesn't have to stoop while working. Wide, deep marble sinks have arching spigots that allow easy access. Cupboards are mahogany finished with low-luster Danish oil.

Handsome materials allow a home office to blend quietly into the decor of a much-used sitting room (opposite). The desktop, right, is made of a pine board covered in Scotchguarded linen and finished with upholstery tacks. It rests on a pair of adjustable 1920s cast-iron stands. A rolling cart can be stored under the desk when not in use. The keyboard tray, above right, is a piece of scrap lumber screwed onto a sliding mechanism from an office-supply catalog. The linen keyboard cover was modeled after a plastic one from an office store. Above, the tangle of wires and cords is suspended in a wire basket hung from cup hooks screwed into the underside of the desk.

LEFT A home office needn't be sequestered from the day-to-day activities of a household. This bright attic combines work space for adults with a playroom for children. Office furniture makes the most of awkward angles; shelves are tailored to fit beneath the eaves, a desk tucks into a dormer. At the heart of the room is a comfortable spot for a midday break: a French campaign chair from the 1880s outfitted with soft new cushions. White paint used on ceiling, walls, and floor makes the room feel airy rather than claustrophobic. Inexpensive shelves, above, are painted in white enamel to match. Archival boxes store papers as neatly as any file cabinet and are labeled for easy identification. A mesh fly cover reveals mail piling up inside.

Professional furniture can often do a multitude of jobs. A stainless-steel table from a restaurant-supply store was cut to size to become a desk that fits snugly within a window alcove (above left). A rolling storage unit fits below. It's made from a vintage metal cabinet outfitted with new wheels. Inexpensive bamboo blinds are lowered halfway to block glare without shutting out an inspiring view. Small boxes designed for CD storage, left, are a perfect fit for computer discs. They are painted white and lined up on a shallow shelf beneath the eaves. Bulldog clips hang from cup hooks screwed into the wall, top right, becoming an impromptu bulletin board. Electric cords, above right, are held by a simple sleeve made by attaching Velcro to a strip of cotton duck.

A quietly chic home office in the corner of a guest bedroom converts easily into a writing desk when visitors come to stay. Cube shelves display a collection of Japanese teapots and also provide storage for office supplies. The laptop computer fits neatly into the space beneath the shelves. Two wooden boxes were constructed to fit exactly in the lowest cubes; felt glued to the bottom lets them slide in and out easily. One holds current files, the other, shown above, is divided into sections for office supplies. Panels of homosote covered in linen are attached to the back of select cubes for tacking up pictures and notes. The desk is a farm table fitted with a leather blotter. A $25 chrome desk chair from the 1970s was reupholstered in a stylish decorator fabric. A utilitarian file cabinet was stripped with paint remover, buffed with steel wool, then finished with an acrylic sealer to prevent rusting.

THIS PAGE AND OPPOSITE Martha
found space for an efficient little office in the
corner of a tight hallway in her New York City
apartment. State-of-the-art electronics look
surprisingly at home alongside sumptuous
tiger-maple veneer shelves and Siena Giallo
marble floors. The wall of shelves ends thirty
inches above the floor in a wide ledge that
doubles as a desktop. A built-in keyboard tray
disappears beneath a slight overhang. A
French desk lamp provides task light, while a
glass lantern overhead illuminates the space.
A cane occasional chair is substantial yet light.
The printer, right, sits atop a rolling file; a felt
pad beneath it prevents scuffs. CD-ROMs,
above, are color-coded by subject. A collection
of copper lustreware pitchers holds pencils,
paper clips, and other common office clutterers.

Walls

More than just a background to a room's decor, walls have a character all their own. Walls may embrace you in an envelope of comfort or appear to expand outward toward the horizon. Using certain techniques and materials, you can emphasize the

polished flatness of a wall or articulate its architecture, and add rhythm and highlights through carefully placed artwork or decorative objects.

The beauty of any wall begins with its smooth and silky flatness, a quality that seems so obvious it often gets overlooked. But take a close look at those around you. Chances are, they're marred by bulges, cracks, and dimples, or else are so mechanically flat they seem altogether lifeless. That's because most interior walls are made of either plaster or drywall. Plaster, used extensively before 1945 and only rarely since then, is troweled on over a skeleton of wooden lath, then sanded smooth. It creates

a beautiful baking-powder finish but tends to crack and buckle with time, and few craftsmen know how to repair it anymore. Drywall is a factory-made panel of gypsum plaster sandwiched between paper layers, hung on a support of wooden or metal studs. While easier and cheaper to install and maintain, it lacks plaster's soft, tactile quality. Plaster is also cool to the touch, since it retains as much as 50 percent water even when dry. To combine the best of both techniques, install three-quarter-inch blueboard, a drywall with a treated surface that allows it to bond with plastering compound. Then skim-coat the surface: Apply three layers of the compound by hand, sanding in between. The final wall is less fragile than plaster but has some of its gentle, animate qualities.

Perfect walls, like any works of art, require a suitable frame, and moldings will articulate their size and shape. The four most common moldings are baseboards, which

OPPOSITE The walls of Martha Stewart's New York City apartment are finished in Swedish putty, a smooth, stonelike material that can hold its own against other strong elements: Siena Giallo marble floors, nickel-plated radiator grille, and a 1940s limed-oak screen. A Warren McArthur armchair sits between a contemporary chrome lamp and an aluminum-leaf bench.

edge a room at floor level and hide the seam where floor meets wall; chair rails, placed approximately three and a half feet off the floor and traditionally used to keep furniture from scuffing walls; picture rails, a foot or more below the ceiling, from which art may be suspended on chains or wires; and crown molding, at the intersection of wall and ceiling. Wainscoting covers the lower third (or more) of walls. It's most appropriate in highly trafficked areas such as kitchens and halls, since it was originally designed to protect walls from scrapes and stains.

Because wooden molding can simply be tacked in place with finishing nails, it's a great way to add instant character to a blank box of a room, but its use should be governed by a sense of propriety and caution. A postwar home with its low ceilings and minimalist walls will merely seem to be masquerading as something it's not if it's dressed in moldings from another era. Look in architectural history books for styles appropriate to the year your home was built if you're uncertain how to proceed.

Moldings do more than add period character. They can also hide flaws and balance misproportions, tricking the eye into reading space differently. A chair rail, for example, can widen a narrow space by emphasizing its horizontal qualities; a picture rail lowers a high ceiling. Similar effects can be produced with paint.

Beautiful as they are, newly minted walls seem a bit cold and impersonal without the addition of art and decorative elements, such as sconces, mirrors, and collections of plates or other objects. And though it can be painful to hammer the first nail into a perfect expanse of wall, it's often even harder to know when to stop. Not every blank wall needs to be covered with something, any more than every silence in a conversation must be filled with mindless chatter. Contrasting open wall space with carefully placed art and accessories gives greater impact to each.

The old rule of picture-hanging was that everything should be suspended at eye level. But while this makes sense in an art gallery, it strikes the wrong chord in a domestic interior. Such an approach makes art seem to exist in its own world, hovering above the life of the room below. A more lively, interesting space can be created if art and decorative objects are arranged in relation to furnishings in their immediate area—so that an inspiring picture perches above a desk, a silvery photograph counterbalances a graceful side chair, and a collection of lustreware plates repeats the sensual curve of a sofa back.

Mirrors, too, can benefit from unconventional placement. A narrow one hung at table height reflects dinnertime candlelight; a large one resting on a mantelpiece can be tilted back so that light from windows bounces upward off its surface, filling the air above with brightness.

A large work of art should hang alone, but smaller masterpieces often work best in groups. Clustering similar objects creates a satisfying pattern, like a mosaic. Before hanging the first one, lay them all out on the floor, where you can shift them around until you're satisfied with the arrangement. Attach the center object to the wall first, followed by the rest in a widening grid around it.

Finally, wall decorations needn't always be predictable. Since Martha can't own the fine paintings she adores, she doesn't settle for reproductions. She visits her beloved Renoirs and van Goghs at the museum, and brings home a vintage stuffed fish from a flea market to grace her East Hampton walls.

OPPOSITE A gilded mirror opens up the wall space above a nineteenth-century marble mantel and reflects light from the room's sole window onto the ceiling. It also frames the hand-painted silk and crystal-bead light fixture, a reproduction of one that Mario Fortuny designed for his palazzo in Venice. The fireplace is carved in a "very crazy patriotic design," according to Martha, who inherited it when she bought the apartment.

ABOVE LEFT A wall beside a staircase is a good place to hang a collection of family photographs that might look static in a boxy room. A single frame color allows the photographs to be appreciated as a graphic pattern when viewed from a distance. Paint can be used to correct awkward room proportions. Horizontal lines lead the eye around a slim and undistinguished space, visually widening it (left). The thickness and spacing of the stripes were determined by the window's measurements. A marble-topped sewing table serves as a desk. In the bedroom above, a painted border lowers a high ceiling. The American-primitive plant table has a lipped lead top. OPPOSITE "It makes a peculiar, loud statement," says Martha of the nineteenth-century stuffed tarpon that decorates her East Hampton library. It suits the house's period, the 1870s, when Victorian taxidermy was at its height. With such dramatic wall decorations, it's best to leave nearby walls bare for contrast.

ABOVE Walls that have no details tend to meld into ceilings and floors, appearing both shorter and closer to one another than they really are. In this plainspoken living room, long, narrow panels painted a darker shade of green than the base color of the walls entice the eye upward. Such a paint treatment also creates visual interest in a sparsely furnished room. Though austere, the Mission chair and stool have a strong geometric presence; faint stripes in the muslin Roman shade and bleached bouclé sisal carpet softly echo the furniture's lines. OPPOSITE Eight-inch stripes painted in two coats of watery pink raise a low ceiling by luring the eye up and down a living-room wall. The color was chosen to match a stripe in the hearth of the turn-of-the-century fireplace. Mercury-glass vases hold roses cut from the garden.

HOW TO PUTTY A WALL

The living-room walls of Martha Stewart's New York City apartment are finished with Swedish putty, a substance so durable it is used to fill holes on the decks of fishing boats in the North Sea. Historically, *enduit*, as it's known in Europe, was used to treat walls before painting a mural or fresco because it yields a perfectly smooth, stonelike surface.

Swedish putty is made of finely ground stone in a binder similar to marine varnish. It can be applied to interior and exterior surfaces; to wood, plaster, drywall, even steel to smooth out any imperfections. Untinted putty is light gray. Pigments can be added to match any color, according to John Lahey, owner of Fine Paints of Europe in Woodstock, Vermont, which distributes the product in the United States. But they should be added by a professional—it takes an hour for a machine to evenly mix pigment into the putty.

Puttying a wall is not easy; it requires a certain level of expertise. First, a special high-tooth priming undercoat is painted on and allowed to dry overnight. Putty can be thinned with linseed oil to slow the drying time. The putty is generously applied to a hawk, a stainless-steel palette with a handle. (Make sure all tools used with the putty are made of stainless steel or aluminum, as any other metal will leave stains.) Using the largest trowel possible, apply a very thin (⅛ inch), smooth coat to the entire surface as you would apply a spackling compound. Allow putty to dry for twenty-four hours before sanding. This first layer of putty should be sanded smooth with a pole sander and 150-grit sandpaper. Remove the dust by wiping down the walls with a tacking cloth (available at paint stores). Repeat the process for the second and third coats, but sand walls each time with finer grit (220 and 320) sandpaper. The process is time-consuming and expensive, but Martha's walls will look as good in fifty years as they do today. To care for the walls, polish with beeswax or Butcher's Wax. Rewax as necessary.

HOW TO PANEL A ROOM

The most important step in painting a paneled room like the one on page 118 is to create a problem-solving design. After sketching possible schemes on paper, mount strips of thick masking tape on the wall and stand back to see whether yours does its job. Apply the base color and let dry overnight. 1 Measure out your scheme, using a metal ruler and a sharp pencil. Make dots at panel corners and every few inches along their edges. To speed measuring, put tape marks on the ruler at frequently measured distances, such as panel widths. 2 Mask around panels, connecting dots with paper painter's tape. Run a fingernail firmly over tape edge to seal. (To make tape removal easier, mask lines that run in the same direction at the same time.) 3 Paint panels, working from the center out with multidirectional brush strokes. Stipple paint around tape edges, then stroke over stippling for thorough coverage. 4 Pull up tape. If paint has run underneath, touch up when panel is dry with the base color and a small artist's brush.

HOW TO PAINT VERTICAL STRIPES

The soft-edged watery pink stripes shown on page 119 work to raise a low ceiling by drawing the eye up and down the wall. The stripes were painted without tape guides. This subtle effect is mistake-proof if you use water-based—or latex—paint, as you can easily remove any stray marks by blotting with a damp cloth. 1 Lightly measure out stripes over a clean, dry base color, using a very sharp pencil and a right angle. Thin down the stripe color using one part paint to two parts water. With a well-blotted brush, paint on stripes up to, but not touching, the pencil lines. 2 If the paint goes on too heavily, wipe it off with a damp rag made from an old T-shirt. To build depth, brush on a second thinned coat over the first one after it's dry. (The first coat will take several hours or overnight to dry.) After you have applied the second coat and allowed it to dry, erase the pencil lines, again using a damp T-shirt rag. To avoid smudging the stripes, change to a clean spot on the rag every few inches.

Transform a favorite corner of the backyard into a place of repose by tying an ordinary tarp from the hardware store onto the trees with lengths of rope. Pierce the tarp with grommet holes to let in pinpoints of sunlight, and set a rustic bench beneath. OPPOSITE Morning is the best time to take in the sun on a porch shuttered against midday heat. A steamer chair was designed for the era of transatlantic crossings, when relaxing was a stylish proposition. Three cushions were covered in ice-cream-colored outdoor fabric and hinged together with Velcro. The covers can be removed and rinsed with a hose.

Relaxing

How to create places where you can put up your feet and let down your hair

EVERYONE NEEDS A PLACE TO ESCAPE TO, A PLACE WHERE THE PETTY cares of the world won't follow. It doesn't have to be far away. Although a weekend house is the ideal retreat, a relaxing spot can be anything from a cushion laid out on the beach to a deck chair plunked down in an overgrown corner of the backyard. It's the grown-up version of a childhood tree house. And just as in those days, imagination can turn it into a palace.

Creating such a place from scratch doesn't require much of an investment. As long as the furniture is sturdy and accommodating, it can be quite humble. Simple chairs and benches from a tag sale or flea market, with or without a fresh coat of paint, invite exactly the kind of put-your-feet-up behavior that's expected of such spots—and that makes them such a relief from formal indoor rooms. With the addition of a few neatly tailored soft goods, rough-hewn furnishings can become surprisingly plush: comfortable cushions to pad hard surfaces, a plump pillow for back support, and a canopy or umbrella to fend off the heat of the summer sun. Made from the newest outdoor fabrics, these things can be as water-, sun-, and salt-resistant as their plastic predecessors without turning sticky on humid days, clammy in cool weather, or mildewed during the course of the winter. And the best of these new acrylic fabrics come in colors and patterns that make them as restful on the eyes as they are on the body.

As for arranging the space, it's best to leave it at least partly up to chance. Chairs should be able to change direction to take advantage of the shifting sun, a canopy set up wherever shade is called for, and everything pulled inside if thunderclouds roll in. After all, the perfect escape zone isn't governed by any predetermined plan. It can invite morning coffee one day and reading, writing, or shelling peas the next. And it's always ready to welcome the most sacred task of all: doing absolutely nothing.

It's hard to beat the simple design of furniture made for city parks and campgrounds when furnishing your own backyard. LEFT A picnic table can sit outside all summer long without showing wear and tear, but its hard seats make for uncomfortable perching. Soften the benches with padded cushions: Cut two-inch-thick urethane foam to size using an electric knife or bread knife; cover with all-weather fabric and attach Velcro-lined straps to hold the cushions in place. A pair of director's chairs is fitted with a similar fabric. BELOW A metal Parisian park chair slips into something more comfortable. A fabric envelope padded with Dacron batting slides over the back; flaps and ties keep the seat cushion in place.

Outdoor spaces shouldn't be governed by too rigid a sense of purpose. A sturdy bench, above, can welcome any number of pastimes, from an afternoon read to an evening courtship. Cushions of urethane foam wrapped in Dacron batting are covered with panels of sea-blue and oyster outdoor fabric. A commodious porch, top right, conveys a timeless sense of grace. A paddle fan suspended from a sky-blue ceiling keeps the breezes moving. A porch swing, right, suspended from the branches of a grand old tree becomes a refuge from phones, faxes, and chores. A vintage curtain and old ticking are recycled as pillow covers. The seat pad is filled with batting and quilted in a diamond pattern.

There's nothing like defying social convention to remind you that you've escaped from the strictures of workaday life. An outdoor shower is exposed yet private. Any secluded spot, outfitted with simple plumbing and hardware, can be transformed into a place to rinse off. A wooden mat, opposite, is sunk into the ground above a pit of pebbles—the only clue to an outdoor shower concealed by a mass of mature Boston ivy. A café chair serves as shower seat and towel rack. A limestone column holds the bare necessities: a natural sponge, a good-sized bar of biodegradable soap, and a brush. THIS PAGE A pile of oak logs is stacked in a U-shape and braced at the corners with four-by-four posts and heavy wire to create a shower camouflaged as a wood pile. Hollow logs supply ventilation, a salvaged beam makes a rough-hewn seat, and irregular logs provide ledges for soap and candles. The shower is disassembled at the end of each summer and burned through fall and winter; fresh logs from tree clearing replace it each spring.

ABOVE AND OPPOSITE With a weekend house, relaxing becomes a familiar ritual. Every Friday night Anita Calero, a photographer and stylist, pulls into the gravel driveway of her house in the Springs, two and a half hours from New York City, and her mind-set shifts. "It's very peaceful," she says of the simple glass box built by an architect for his own use in 1969. Shortly after buying it in 1994, she was inspired to have a deck constructed at the edge of the clearing surrounding the house. "When I closed my eyes I could imagine it," she says, "and when I opened them it was there." Calero now refers to it as "the island," and it has become the focus of summer entertaining. Constructed of two-by-fours propped up on a foundation of wooden posts, it combines a civilized attitude with a summer-camp setting. Calero combines simplicity and elegance in her table settings, too. "I like basic things," she says. "White, with touches of color in the napkins, really good glasses and really good silver." The tablecloth is plain white paper, smooth as linen but easy to throw away after a meal. The cherry-red chairs are French forties bistro. The steel table is by designer Mary Adams; an identical table sits indoors.

"The size of the house is perfect," says Calero. "It's so small and easy to maintain." Endless windows on two sides dissolve the walls and make it feel vast despite its size. The space—a living and dining area with an open kitchen along one end—was designed by Calero's friend Lora Zarubin. Café chairs and a trestle bench provide seating at the table. The living area is defined by a 1950s American woven-paper carpet; the armchairs are French, from the 1940s. A paper lamp designed by Isamu Noguchi is a sculptural source of ambient lighting. OPPOSITE An ashwood partition serves as a back for the velvet-covered sofa, designed by Calero. It also sets off the kitchen, where the house's original cabinets make a colorful mural. The kitchen (left) is fitted with restaurant equipment; the countertop is an old piece of ship's lumber.

Strong horizontal lines used throughout the design of Calero's house give it a laid-back air, dramatically different from the city's vertical rhythm. Calero designed the low open storage system, above left. Made of Philippine mahogany, it's propped on iron legs that she had cast at a foundry. An assortment of boxes holds favorite things. Calero chose images of nature from her collection of photographs to decorate this house, leaving more graphic pictures back in the city. In the guest bedroom, above, crisp light linens and plain wood surfaces create a feeling of calm. Calero's eye for exquisite detail extends even to the curtain hooks, left, created as a gift by jewelry designer Ted Muehling. In the bedroom opposite, stacks of plain white pillows provide support for bedtime reading. The duvet cover is made from antique fabric; the curtains are antique cotton mattress ticking found in the south of France. The bedside lamp base is a wooden Italian saint. The ink-on-paper work by David Carrino is a stylization of famous literary autographs.

In the shelter of a weeping willow, a hanging canopy reflects light inwards, creating an illusion of enclosure beneath an open sky. (See page 138 for instructions.) Rattan porch chairs from the 1940s are moved to the lawn for dinner. The table is set all in white, with ironstone dishes and a linen cloth. A stainless-steel ship's lantern hangs from a rope hooked onto the center of the canopy. OPPOSITE A panel canopy creates a place to pause just outside a kitchen door. It's made from translucent plastic mesh and wooden poles painted with stripes (see page 139 for instructions). Beneath it, nineteenth-century French park chairs and a blue metal café table are joined by a turn-of-the-century farmer's chair from Sweden.

HOW TO MAKE A HANGING CANOPY

An old tree is its own world of shade. A suspended canopy (shown set for dinner by lamplight on page 136) can provide a place within that world—a kind of tree house hung low. Four linked canvas panels hung from the tree and staked to the ground create shelter without impeding the tree's shadows. In fact, they enhance them: The panels display leafy pictures, like projection screens. 1 The basis of the canopy is a frame of four wooden dowels, hooked together into a square that hangs from a tree bough. Each 5-by-10-foot canvas panel is hemmed along one of the short edges to create a channel for a dowel that is 2 inches in diameter and 5 feet long. The dowels are laid out in a square, with the canvas panels extending away. 2 A screw eye is attached to both ends of each dowel. The square frame that the four dowels form is held together by two 8-foot lengths of nylon clothesline with metal snap hooks tied to each end. Each of the four snap hooks clips onto the screw eyes at the ends of two dowels, connecting one dowel to the next to link them into a square. The nylon lines tied to the snap hooks are run diagonally across the square, corner to corner. Before being hooked to its opposite corner, each line is passed through a heavy metal ring. 3 The ring is snap-hooked to a 30-foot length of 3-strand, ⅜-inch nautical line, which runs up through a standard pulley hung on a strong, short chain from the bough. 4 The other end of the 30-foot line runs down from the pulley to a metal cleat fixed to the tree trunk at waist height, where the line is secured. With the pulley and extra line, the canopy can be raised and lowered easily. 5 The frame and panels are raised by pulling the line through the pulley. The nylon lines of the frame should form a taut, level pyramid when the canopy is suspended. Before winding the pulley line around the cleat, stand under the frame to decide the ceiling height you want. 6 The bottom end of each panel is turned over 2 inches and hemmed, with a grommet at each corner. 7 Two-foot lengths of line are hooked onto the corner grommets with nautical snap shackles and staked to hold the panels taut in wide, tentlike wings. 8 Suspended from the boughs of a weeping willow, the canopy creates a quiet enclave for reading or talking in the dappled afternoon light.

HOW TO MAKE A PANEL CANOPY

Multiple panels of awning material suspended close together (see page 137) are lighter and allow a greater area of coverage than a single awning. They also permit a greater play of breeze beneath, and festoon the house like banners. The panels are supported by wooden poles (those shown here are 3 feet tall and 3 inches in diameter) striped gondola-style and topped with curtain finials. The three panels shown—more can easily be added to the design—are 2-by-12-foot lengths of Textilene, a polyester-mesh awning material. 1 One of the short (2 foot) edges of each panel is turned over 2 inches and hemmed. Six turn fasteners (they look like grommets) are inserted in the hem; two together at each corner for strength, and two single ones spaced evenly in between. 2 The turn-fastener ends of the panels are screwed, through the turn-fastener

holes, onto existing trim on the wall, about 10 feet above the ground. 3 The opposite end of each panel is hemmed, and a grommet inserted at each corner just above the hem. Screw eyes are inserted in the poles near the top, just below the finials. Snap hooks are clipped to the grommets in the panel corners and to the screw eyes on the poles. 4 A 1-foot 6-inch length of standard PVC plumbing pipe is used to hold the poles in the ground. For each pole, a 1-foot 6-inch hole is dug, 2 inches wider than the PVC pipe. The pipe is centered in the hole and the post inserted in the pipe. (This way, when the canopy is taken down, the posts are simply pulled out of the pipes.) The posts are tilted outward to prevent the panels from pulling back and collapsing the canopy. The hole is then filled with gravel to secure the tilted pole.

Floors

It's easy to overlook floors. They don't confront you when you walk into a room the way a striking painting or armchair might. Yet they affect the character of a space profoundly. The same arrangement of furniture looks entirely different if it sits on an expanse of marble tiles, on polished wood boards, or on a patterned wool carpet.

Floors are probably the largest surfaces you have to contend with when decorating a room, and because they must be durable and strong as well as beautiful, resurfacing them can be quite expensive. Yet good floors are a wise investment, because they don't go out of style. The most common materials and finishes have been used for centuries and will outlast the next fifty design trends. They include wood, stone, and tile, with or without treatments and coverings such as carpets, rugs, and paint. WOOD The first wood floors were simply the ceilings of the rooms below, and were so rough and raw that sand was rubbed into them to clean them. Such grit is anathema to the polished wood floors we prize today—a single pebble caught in the sole of a shoe can leave behind a web of scars. But with a little care, wood floors can be among the most satisfying choices to live with.

Wood has great sensuality and warmth. Light reflected off it lends a burnished glow to all the other objects in a room. And the slight undulations and imperfections in its grain give it a movement and vitality that other hard, flat surfaces often lack. Floor boards may be made either of hardwood, such as oak or maple, or softwood, such as pine or fir. As the names imply, hardwoods are less likely to scratch and dent, but they are also considerably more expensive than softwoods. Either kind may be cut into simple strips or interlocking tongue-and-groove boards—they can also be bleached or stained to

OPPOSITE A floor painted in a simple geometric pattern seems to enlarge a small home office tucked into an attic. A muted palette and pale, silvery furnishings further the airy feeling: The 1960s stainless-steel desk is typical of the American industrial style; the 1950s Scandinavian reading chair is woven wicker and stainless steel.

acquire any color from ash-blond to coffee brown (wood stains, like paint, can be custom-mixed for greater character and intensity). Wood floors must be sealed to protect them from moisture and abrasion. The newest water-based urethane finishes are tougher, less toxic, and less likely to yellow than traditional varnishes. They also create a deep, rich sheen that glows like the surface of a lake.

STONE Marble, slate, and granite have a monumental quality that recalls plazas, cathedrals, and great civic buildings. No wonder stone seems more at home in transitional spaces such as foyers and hallways than in private bedrooms and sitting rooms. Its durability and earthiness also make stone flooring suitable for utilitarian rooms such as kitchens and baths. Once too massive to be used anywhere in houses but on the ground floor, stone can now be cut into tile-thin squares which can be laid almost anywhere. Most stone is porous and will stain and discolor with age unless sealed. It also becomes dangerously slippery if polished rather than honed or etched. Stone will always be cold to the touch, but for sheer opulence and grandeur, it is unparalleled.

TILE Cement, porcelain, clay, glass, and even asphalt can be formed into tiles, a good choice for bathroom and kitchen floors because they are sanitary and waterproof. Tiles add rhythm as well as color to a room: Tiny octagonal tiles create a light mosaic, larger ones a more sedate geometry. Glazed tiles are slippery and should be used for floors only if they have an uneven or textured surface, or if the tiles are small enough that the grout between them creates a nonslip pattern.

RUGS AND CARPETS The finest antique Oriental rugs can be as precious as the most valuable works of art in any museum. But floor coverings of such value are a bit paralyzing to live with—you hardly dare breathe in their vicinity. More comfortable are contemporary rugs and carpets that balance beauty with durability. The best material is wool, which outlasts all synthetics and other natural fibers, naturally repels dirt, and becomes more beautiful with age. But a wool carpet isn't invincible, and will suffer if used in high-traffic areas, under chairs that are constantly dragged back and forth, or near doorways where dirt and debris are brought in from outside.

A good rug should be surrounded by at least a foot of bare floor on all sides, to frame it like a piece of art. Smaller rugs can be used to define spaces within a large room, such as a conversation area set off on its own little island. A rug at the end of a long hallway or beneath a chair in the corner of a country kitchen can also announce that you've arrived at a place of rest and repose.

PAINT Paint is one of the quickest and cheapest ways to fix less-than-perfect floors and add character and dignity to a room. When properly applied and sealed (see pages 150 and 151), paint is easy to care for, takes on a soft, rubbed-down look as it wears, and can be touched up in minutes if necessary. An ordinary hardware store sells everything needed to create painted floors yourself.

Painted floors have a long—if not exactly venerable—history. For centuries they were used by ordinary folks to mimic the floors of the aristocracy. There was faux marble in Renaissance Italy, imitation carpets in eighteenth-century Sweden, and fake parquetry in Georgian England. These days, painted floors are simply practical and pretty. An all-white floor appears to enlarge a room, and draws attention to any furniture starkly outlined against it. A more richly colored floor can unify disparate elements of a decorating scheme, and envelop a room in a calm hush. And a painted-on pattern can lend a lively underpinning to an ordinary space. Whichever you choose, you'll be happy to know there's something wonderful happening underfoot.

In Martha Stewart's East Hampton house, fir planks are stained a deep coffee color to go with her dark walnut and mahogany furniture. The stain, a mixture of five different pigments, is sealed with two coats of water-based urethane, then finished with clear bowling-alley wax. The floors are buffed once a month to maintain their deep luster. A marble-topped Charles X table is flanked by a pair of chairs upholstered in glazed linen.

OPPOSITE Floors, unlike walls, can handle bold and colorful pattern without making a room feel crowded. A nineteenth-century ingrain carpet spreads out beneath a mahogany-veneer gaming table and a quartet of Georgian-style chairs. Such carpets were popular a century ago; made from two interlocking layers of woven wool, they are reversible, with colors and patterns transposed on opposite sides. RIGHT On a sunporch, afternoon light stretches across an ingrain carpet patterned with large medallions. BELOW RIGHT An 1850s ingrain carpet softens a bedroom decorated with a Sheraton-style bed and nineteenth-century sewing table. Ingrains were usually installed wall to wall, but this one is centered to show off its acanthus-leaf border. BELOW A Gothic Revival carpet features the crosses and trefoils typical of the style. Worn-out ingrain carpets can be cut up to make pillows, hall or table runners, or bedspreads.

In a dining room reminiscent of a Swedish summer house, a pale gingham floor makes a sly allusion to traditional checkerboard tiles. Its lime-sherbet palette is echoed on the painted walls. The floor was created by Eve Ashcraft, a paint and color specialist in New York City (see page 150 for instructions). Spare but graceful furnishings add to the room's charming delicacy. The reproduction dining chairs are painted dove gray. A pair of simple ironstone platters forms the only overmantel decoration. Plain linen roller shades soften summer light. OPPOSITE Ashcraft adapted the traditional folk-art technique of combing to create a basket-weave pattern on a painted bedroom floor. The base color, Pratt & Lambert Osprey #1292, was allowed to dry, then a second coat of tinted glazing liquid was applied and dragged off in alternating directions with a rubber comb. Because the two colors are close in tone, the effect is of a softly textured surface rather than a strong pattern. A daybed from the 1920s catches the cool light from a northern window.

OPPOSITE Handmade Mexican tiles give depth and vitality to the floor of Martha's East Hampton kitchen. Teal-green pigment was pressed into the wet cement as the tiles were made; they were then air-dried and hand-polished. The top of the custom-made table is composed of two pieces of marble; its sturdy wooden legs are reminiscent of Mission furniture. Martha found the fourteen matching grange chairs in Maine; they are stained rather than painted, so the color of the wood shows through. THIS PAGE A faux finish gives a pine floor oak graining. There's no attempt at deception, though; the edges of the painted "boards" don't match the real ones beneath, and the color contrast is heightened to announce the mimicry. Teeny, one of Martha's Himalayan cats, peers down from the safe distance of a painted Hitchcock chair. A bowl of Araucana eggs sits on a zinc-topped farm table nearby.

STRIPING AND GINGHAM PATTERN

1 To paint a border, stripes (above), or the quadrant on page 140, measure the desired widths on the floor with a tape measure; mark with yellow dot stickers. Outline the space with painter's tape. 2 With a bristle brush, paint evenly between tape borders, overlapping edges of tape by roughly ½". 3 Remove tape and let dry. When dry, reapply tape along edge of painted area and apply next color. Continue until floor is completed.

To create the gingham floor pictured on page 146 and below, you'll need to refer to the templates on page 157. First, measure the dimensions of your floor and make a scale drawing to work from. The width of each gingham square is based on these measurements. For example, if your floor measures 15' by 20', you will create three hundred 1' squares (fifteen across and twenty deep). Disregard the width of the floorboards when measuring. 1 Paint specialist Eve Ashcraft assembles her equipment: a bucket of glaze, a roll of brown painter's tape, a 4"-wide foam applicator for the squares, a nylon bristle brush for the border, color swatches of glazes she tested on pieces of heavy white cardboard, a metal ruler, and her scale drawing of the pattern (see template #1). The floor is first painted with the base color, Pratt & Lambert Silver Lin-

ing #2288, and allowed to dry. Following the scale drawing, Ashcraft marks the floor with yellow dot stickers to designate the width of the gingham bands. She then lays painter's tape in strips to connect the stickers, outlining squares that are to be painted first. 2 Using a foam applicator, she applies a dark-green glaze to outlined squares. The painter's tape will overlap adjacent squares, which will be glazed later in a lighter green. Immediately after glazing the darker green squares, Ashcraft removes tape from the right and left sides of each square. 3 Once the glaze has dried, she uses tape to outline the unglazed squares to the right and left of the darker green squares (tape will overlap the already glazed squares; see template #2). She applies a lighter green to the unglazed squares, then removes all the tape, revealing bands of alternating dark- and light-green squares. 4 Ashcraft uses tape to outline the unglazed squares above and below the painted dark-green squares (see template #3) and glazes these areas in a light green. She then tapes out the border that will run around the edge of the gingham pattern (see template #4). Ashcraft glazes this border in turquoise. Once it's completed, she lets the whole floor dry overnight, then seals it with a water-based floor sealer, Varathane Satin.

WOOD GRAINING

The wood pattern for this floor (pictured above and on page 149) is made by covering a painted or natural surface with glaze and then using a patterning tool to remove some of the glaze. 1 To apply the *faux bois*, or false wood, graining to a pine floor, Ashcraft uses a 5"-wide wood-graining roller from an arts-and-crafts store. The width of this tool will determine the width of the painted "planks." She uses a metal ruler with a yellow dot at 5" to mark off the floor. The first plank to be glazed is outlined with blue painter's tape. The edges of the tape are firmly pressed down to ensure a tight seal. 2 Once the area has been outlined, Ashcraft uses a 2" nylon brush to apply a glaze made by mixing water-based glazing liquid and universal tints. 3 Starting at one end of the taped-off plank, Ashcraft drags and rolls the wood-grainer to pattern the glaze. If mistakes are made, they can be corrected with a pencil eraser, or glaze can be wiped off and reapplied. (If necessary, practice on scrap wood until you feel proficient.) As the plank dries, Ashcraft tapes off and glazes one that is not adjacent to the freshly painted one. The whole process takes several days. 4 The trompe l'oeil oak plank doesn't match up with the pine board beneath; the idea isn't really to deceive the eye, but to please it.

COMBING

To achieve the basket-weave pattern pictured below and page 147, Ashcraft adapted the traditional folk-art technique of combing. Like wood graining, it involves covering a surface with glaze, then using a patterning tool to remove some of the glaze. 1 Ashcraft begins by painting the floor with a base coat of Pratt & Lambert's Osprey #1292. After it has dried overnight, she uses a foam applicator to apply a tinted glazing liquid to a workable area, about 20" by 20". 2 She then uses a handmade 5"-wide rubber comb to remove some of the glaze in alternating directions, forming a basket-weave pattern. Between combings, excess glaze is wiped off on a cloth. The width of the pattern is determined by the size of the comb. Ashcraft made hers of industrial rubber, because she wanted it to be more flexible than the metal combs used by folk artists. As each 20"-by-20" area is finished, Ashcraft removes the glaze around the edges with a damp cloth and moves on to a new area. Mistakes are corrected and the pattern continued in difficult spaces with a pencil eraser, which Ashcraft calls "a one-toothed comb." When the glaze has dried for twenty-four hours, two coats of Varathane Diamond Finish satin sealer are applied to seal the floor.

Guide

Items pictured but not listed are from private collections. Addresses and telephone numbers of sources are correct as of April 1996 but are subject to change, as are the price and availability of any item.

COVER
Martha Stewart's SWEATERS by Calvin Klein, PANTS from J.Crew.

COLOR
pages 10 to 31
INTERIOR PAINTERS Eve Ashcraft Studio, 247 Centre Street, New York, NY 10013; 212-966-1506. Luis J. León, Box 536, Wainscott, NY 11975; 516-329-2326. Dennis Rowan Services, 250 Post Road East, Westport, CT 06880; 203-227-6488. PAINT Araucana Colors, $75 for 2.5 liters, Colors from the Garden, $24 for 750 milliliters, $70 for 2.5 liters, both from Fine Paints of Europe, Box 419, Woodstock, VT 05091; 800-332-1556 for catalog, color chart, and nearest retailer.
pages 12 and 13
FIRE SCREEN from J. Garvin Mecking, 72 East 11th Street, New York, NY 10003; 212-677-4316. To the trade only. DINING CHAIRS, $8,000 for set of 8, and French faience URN and BASIN, $750, both from Pierre Deux Antiques, 369 Bleecker Street, New York, NY 10014; 212-243-7740. Painted COLUMN, $240, from Rooms & Gardens, 290 Lafayette Street, New York, NY 10012; 212-431-1297.
page 16
19th-century French CHAIRS, $3,400 for set of 4, 19th-century PEDESTAL, $480, MARBLE GRAPES, $80 to $120 per bunch, and Jane Johnson SKETCH, $600,

all from Rooms & Gardens, 290 Lafayette Street, New York, NY 10012; 212-431-1297.
page 18
BED, $35, from Sage Street Antiques, Sage Street and Route 114, Sag Harbor, NY 11963; 516-725-4036. Painted BENCH, $1,500, from John Rosselli International, 523 East 73rd Street, New York, NY 10021; 212-772-2137. Chair SLIPCOVER sewn by Ann Baderian Polokoff Ltd., 35-38 164th Street, Flushing, NY 11358; 718-359-0309. TABLE, $2,950, from Pierre Deux Antiques, 369 Bleecker Street, New York, NY 10014; 212-243-7740.
page 21
Large turquoise VASE, $180, from Rooms & Gardens, 290 Lafayette Street, New York, NY 10012; 212-431-1297. Linen damask TABLECLOTH, $250, from Laura Fisher/Antique Quilts & Americana, 1050 Second Avenue, New York, NY 10022; 212-838-2596.
page 22
18th-century French ANDIRONS, $800 for the pair, from Rooms & Gardens, 290 Lafayette Street, New York, NY 10012; 212-431-1297. Framed COLLAGE, $1,000, and driftwood LAMPS, $1,250 per pair, from Bilhuber, 330 East 59th Street, New York, NY 10022; 212-308-4888. Garden TABLE from J. Garvin Mecking, 72 East 11th Street, New York, NY 10003; 212-677-4316. To the trade only. Christian Berard

WATERCOLOR, c. 1940, $5,500, from Liz O'Brien, 41 Wooster Street, New York, NY 10013; 212-343-0935. Verge SIDE CHAIR, $6,350, and ceramic LAMP, $600 to $800, from AERO Ltd., 132 Spring Street, New York, NY 10012; 212-966-1500. Bijoux END TABLE, $5,925, from John Boone, 1059 Third Avenue, New York, NY 10021; 212-758-0012. To the trade only. Noble CHAIR and OTTOMAN from Donghia; 800-366-4442. To the trade only.
page 25
Laurel Haze FLOOR TILES by Astra (style #6004), $8.25 per square foot, from Alan Court & Associates, 57B Main Street, East Hampton, NY 11937; 516-324-7497.
page 31
Universal TINTING COLORS, $5 to $11 per pint, from Merit-Kaplan, 237 East 44th Street, New York, NY 10017; 212-682-3585.

GATHERING
pages 32 to 35
COUNTERS, CABINETS, SHELVES, DRAWERS, CARTS, and TABLES custom-made by Duralab Equipment Corp., 10723 Farragut Road, Brooklyn, NY 11236; 718-649-9600. (All Duralab products are custom-ordered; there is no stock or inventory. Because pieces must be assembled, painted, and shipped, delivery may take some time.) ROOM DESIGN by Walter Chatham Architects, 580 Broadway, Room 1001, New York, NY 10012; 212-925-2202.
page 33
French Consulat Cuban-

mahogany DINING TABLE, $24,000, from Reymer-Jourdan Antiques, 43 East 10th Street, New York, NY 10003; 212-674-4470. Ladder-back dining CHAIRS from Stuart Parr, 67 Vestry Street, New York, NY 10013; 212-431-0732. NAPKINS, $20 each, CHOPSTICKS, $6 per pair, and TEA BOWLS, $35 each, all from Takashimaya, 693 Fifth Avenue, New York, NY 10022; 212-350-0100 or 800-753-2038.
pages 38 and 39
"Swayback" SOFA, $2,998, at Shabby Chic, 93 Greene Street, New York, NY 10012; 212-274-9842. Small silk PILLOWS at ABC Carpet & Home, 888 Broadway, New York, NY 10003; 212-473-3000 or 800-888-7847. Original Heywood-Wakefield COFFEE TABLE, $475, from City Barn Antiques, 362 Atlantic Avenue, Brooklyn, NY 11217; 718-855-8566. Original Heywood-Wakefield RECORD CABINET, $675, from Chris Kennedy, 3 Olive Street, Northampton, MA 01060; 413-584-6804. REPRODUCTION HEYWOOD-WAKEFIELD FURNITURE available from South Beach Furniture/Heywood-Wakefield, 180 N.E. 39th Street, Miami, FL 33137; 305-576-0201.
page 40
Viking ROLLER WINDOW SHADES, about $40 each, from East End Installations, 8 Lloyd Street, Center Moriches, New York, NY 11934; 516-878-9000 or 800-287-4554.
pages 40 and 41
All PAINT from Benjamin Moore. On front sitting-room walls: latex

flat #270 mixed with 50 percent Decorators White. Paint on back sitting-room walls and upstairs hallway: latex flat #270. Paint on dining-room walls: latex flat #307 mixed with Cal-Tint II universal tinting colorant in raw sienna/yellow oxide. Trim paint: eggshell enamel ow-18 (color discontinued, but paint stores can still mix it). Paint on floors: Porch & Floor Enamel in Oxford Blue mixed with low-luster polyurethane. Call 800-826-2623 for nearest retailer.

page 42
Giant glass Chinese APOTHE-CARY JARS with metal lids, $135 each, from H, 335 East Ninth Street, New York, NY 10003; 212-477-2631. Custom-made JACQUARD RUG, $100 per square yard, from Elizabeth Eakins, 21 East 65th Street, New York, NY 10021; 212-628-1950.

pages 42 and 43
Large porcelain FAUCET HAN-DLES, $90, and Old-style Chicago FAUCET, $300, both from A. Ball Plumbing Supply, 1703 West Burnside Street, Portland, OR 97209; 800-228-0134. White glass ceiling and wall LAMPSHADES, $33 each, from Roy Electric Co., 1054 Coney Island Avenue, Brooklyn, NY 11230; 718-434-7002 or 800-366-3347. Brass crescent DRAWER PULLS (#97172), $4.95 each, from Renovator's Supply, Box 2515, Conway, NH 03818; 800-659-2211. Large oval brass CUPBOARD TURNS, (#170C) $34, and brass CABINET HINGES, $20 per pair, both from Crown City Hardware Co., 1047 North Allen Avenue, Pasadena, CA 91104; 818-794-1188. White porcelain DOORKNOBS, $29.95 per pair, and TOWEL BAR, $42.95, both from Antique Hardware & Home, 1C Mathews Court, Hilton Head, SC 29928; 803-681-4987 or 800-422-9982.

page 44
Antique TEA TABLE, $14,000, from Kinnaman & Ramaekers, P.O. BOX 1140, Wainscott, NY 11975; 516-537-0779. GLAZED LINEN (on sofa) by Nicholas Haslam, from Rose Tarlow-

Melrose House, 8454 Melrose Place, Los Angeles, CA 90069; 213-651-2202.

page 45
Rattan ARMCHAIRS, $1,500 each, from Mariette Himes Gomez Associates, 506 East 74th Street, New York, NY 10021; 212-288-6856. Standing EXTENSION-ARM LAMP, $750, from Historical Materialism, 125 Crosby Street, New York, NY 10012; 212-431-3424. Iron Empire CHAIR, $650, from Florentine Craftsmen, 46-24 28th Street, Long Island City, NY 11101; 800-876-3567. Iron SIDE CHAIR, $684, from Treillage Limited, 413 East 75th Street, New York, NY 10021; 212-535-2288. Annapolis Gray CANVAS on chairs (#1005), $47 per yard, from Giati Designs, 614 Santa Barbara Street, Santa Barbara, CA 93101; call 805-965-6535 for nearest showroom. Custom IRON TABLES, $125 for small, $450 for large, from Morgik, 20 West 22nd Street, New York, NY 10010; 212-463-0304. Custom PLASTER TABLE-TOP, $950, by Art in Construction, 8 Beach Street, New York, NY 10013; 212-334-5227. Folk-art SIDE TABLE, $395, from Paula Rubenstein Ltd., 65 Prince Street, New York, NY 10012; 212-966-8954. PURPLE VASE, $60, and STRIPED VASE, $125, from AERO Ltd., 132 Spring Street, New York, NY 10012; 212-966-1500.

page 46
Antique cast-iron TABLE, $2,700, and mahogany SIDE TABLE, $1,800, from Mariette Himes Gomez Associates, 506 East 74th Street, New York, NY 10021; 212-288-6856. Free catalog. Sisal FLOOR COVERING from ABC Carpet & Home, 888 Broadway, New York, NY 10003; 212-473-3000 or 800-888-7847.

page 47
CANVAS CURTAINS in sage with "Caribbean" border, $47 per yard, from Giati Designs, 614 Santa Barbara Street, Santa Barbara, CA 93101; call 805-965-6535 for nearest showroom. LAMP BASE, $195, from David

Stypmann, 192 Sixth Avenue, New York, NY 10013; 212-226-5717. Burlap LAMPSHADES, $29, from Just Shades, 21 Spring Street, New York, NY 10012; 212-966-2757. COIR FLOOR COV-ERING, $27.50 per square yard, from Aronson's, 135 West 17th Street, New York, NY 10011; 212-243-4993.

WINDOWS
page 50
SHADE custom-made by Lisa Hammerquist, 240 Sheridan Avenue, #2w, Albany, NY 12210; 518-434-9151. Gilt CORNICE by Eve Ashcraft Studio, 212-966-1506. Claridge FABRIC (#33030/3) from Clarence House, 211 East 58th Street, New York, NY 10022; 212-752-2890. To the trade only.

page 53
ROMAN SHADES custom-made by Ann Baderian Polokoff Ltd., 35-38 164th Street, Flushing, NY 11358; 718-359-0309. Palazzo TAFFETA (#4910-03), Plato CLUB CHAIR (#2901) covered in Lodz linen (#8601-08), all by Donghia; 800-366-4442. To the trade only.

page 54
ROLLER SHADES and PAPER SHADES (on blue doors), both custom-made by Ann Baderian Polokoff Ltd., 35-38 164th Street, Flushing, NY 11358; 718-359-0309. Edgartown TICKING STRIPE in handwoven cotton (#LFY-10618F), $30 per yard, from the Ralph Lauren Home Collection, 1185 Avenue of the Americas, New York, NY 10036; 212-642-8700.

page 55
ROLL-UP SHADE and BUTTERFLY SHADE, both custom-made by Ann Baderian Polokoff Ltd., 35-38 164th Street, Flushing, NY 11358; 718-359-0309. Orient Express cotton FABRIC in Bleu de France (#33002/29-4A), from Clarence House, 211 East 58th Street, New York, NY 10022; 212-752-2890. To the trade only.

page 56
Top left: Edwardian LINEN SHEET from the Grand Acquisitor, 110 North Main Street, East Hampton, NY 11937; 516-324-

7272. By appointment only. Top right: Cotton THEATRICAL SCRIM, $1.80 per yard, from Rose Brand, 517 West 35th Street, New York, NY 10001; 212-594-7424 or 800-223-1624. Bottom left: Kent Irish handkerchief LINEN, about $24 per yard, from Hamilton Adams Linen. Call 212-221-0800 for retailers. Bottom right: Swedish homespun linen TEA TOWELS, $16 each, from the Grand Acquisitor, see above. Brass CAFÉ CLIPS, $4, from Bed Bath & Beyond, 620 Sixth Avenue, New York, NY 10011; 212-255-3550 for other store locations.

page 57
Hand-carved MAHOGANY BRANCH, $65 per foot (23-karat-gold finish an additional $60 per foot), at Joseph Biunno Ltd., 129 West 29th Street, 2nd floor, New York, NY 10001; 212-629-5630. VELVET LEAVES, $2 each (made to order), at Dulken & Derrick, 12 West 21st Street, New York, NY 10010; 212-929-3614. COTTON SCRIM, 93¢ per yard, at Rose Brand, 517 West 35th Street, New York, NY 10001; 212-594-7424.

page 58
Custom-made WOODEN BLIND by Nanik, 7200 Stewart Avenue, Wausau, WI 54402; 800-422-4544. To the trade only. MATCHSTICK BLIND custom-made by Ann Baderian Polokoff Ltd., 35-38 164th Street, Flushing, NY 11358; 718-359-0309.

page 59
ROMAN SHADE custom-made by Lisa Hammerquist, 240 Sheridan Avenue, #2w, Albany, NY 12210; 518-434-9151. LAROCHE LINEN (used for lower section) in natural (#8609-08) by Donghia; 800-366-4442. To the trade only. YEATES LINEN (used for upper section) in oyster (c-363) from Roger Arlington, 979 Third Avenue, New York, NY 10022; 212-752-5288. To the trade only.

page 60
Custom-made WOODEN BLIND by Nanik, 7200 Stewart Avenue, Wausau, WI 54402; 800-422-4544. To the trade only. (Slat colors, from right to left: Clay #37,

Amethyst #55, Sandstone #111, White #100, Tapestry Teal #60, Muslin #51, Linen #115, Driftwood #2, Sandalwood #53; tape colors: beige, black, tan, and ivory.)

page 61

Kent Irish handkerchief LINEN, about $24 per yard, from Hamilton Adams Linen. Call 212-221-0800 for retailers. Top right: SMALL RINGS by Garouste & Bonetti, $350 each, at Neotu, 409 West 44th Street, New York, NY 10036; 212-262-9250. BRASS RING WITH ARROW at Joseph Biunno Ltd., 129 West 29th Street, 2nd floor, New York, NY 10001; 212-629-5630. BRASS RING WITH LEAF at Piston's Antiques, 1050 Second Avenue, New York, NY 10022; 212-753-8322. Bottom right: METAL RING WITH FLEUR-DE-LIS, $22.50, MAHOGANY RING, $15 (23-karat-gold finish an additional $28.50 each); RINGS, $16.50 each (painted finish an additional $25), all at Joseph Biunno Ltd., see above.

COMFORT

page 62

Goodnight X's queen-size flat SHEET, $192, and standard PILLOWCASE, $120 per pair, both by Angel Zimmick, at Portico Bed & Bath, 139 Spring Street, New York, NY 10012; 212-941-7722. Palm-vegetable-dye PILLOW SHAM with bow from ABC Carpet & Home, 888 Broadway, New York, NY 10003; 212-473-3000. Matelassé BLANKET COVER by Anichini, about $400, from E. Braun & Co., 717 Madison Avenue, New York, NY 10021; 212-838-0650 (or call 800-372-7286 for nearest retailer). Reading #19B Woodard-weave RUG, $13.75 per square foot, from Woodard & Greenstein, 506 East 74th Street, 5th floor, New York, NY 10021; 212-988-2906. Catalog $6. CANOPY sewn by Lisa Hammerquist, 240 Sheridan Avenue, #2W, Albany, NY 12210; 518-434-9151. GINGHAM FABRIC (for boudoir pillow), $4.95 per yard; MEN'S SHIRTING FABRIC (for pillow innercase), $14.95 per yard, both from Rosen & Chadick, 246

West 40th Street, New York, NY 10018; 212-869-0142. Monaco PILLOWS, $36 for boudoir, $90 for standard, $110 for queen, all from Garnet Hill; 800-622-6216.

page 63

Polished-chrome 3-valve SHOWER SET by Speakman, $305, polished-chrome HAND SPRAY SET by Brasstech, $162, City TOWEL BARS by Cropusa, $72 for 18", $77 for 24", Candy Bright White 3"-by-4" SUBWAY TILES, $6.95 per square foot, Kowa ¾" HEXAGONAL TILES, $4 per square foot, all from Alan Court & Associates, 57B Main Street, East Hampton, NY 11937; 516-324-7497.

page 65

Vintage BED LINENS from the Grand Acquisitor, 110 North Main Street, East Hampton, NY 11937; 516-324-7272. By appointment only. Custom-made queen-size HORSEHAIR MATTRESS, $909, from Charles H. Beckley, 749 East 137th Street, Bronx, NY 10454; 718-665-2218. SIDE-TABLE BASES, about $300, from Nellie's of Amagansett, 255 Main Street, Amagansett, NY 11930; 516-267-1000. Custom-made beveled ZINC TOPS from Klatt Sheet Metal, 479 Hubbard Avenue, Aquebogue, NY 11931; 516-722-3515. Painted centennial CHAIRS from Consignmart, 877 Post Road East, Westport, CT 06880; 203-226-0841. Belgian LINEN RUG (cut to size; roll is 13'1" wide), $100 per square yard, from Harmill Carpets, 969 Third Avenue, New York, NY 10022; 212-838-1330. Custom SCREEN FRAME KIT, from Kestrel Manufacturing, P.O. BOX 12, St. Peters, PA 19470-0012; 610-469-6444 or 800-494-4321. ⅛" PASTEL GREEN GLASS by Wiss, $3.75 per square foot, from S. A. Bendheim, 122 Hudson Street, New York, NY 10013; 212-226-6370. White Dove PAINT by Benjamin Moore; 800-826-2623 for nearest dealer. White LINEN, $21.95 per yard, from B & J Fabrics, 263 West 40th Street, New York, NY 10018; 212-354-8150.

pages 66 and 67

TOWEL BAR from Urban Archaeology, 285 Lafayette Street, New York, NY 10012; 212-431-6969. Wall SPONGE HOLDER, $326, and SHOWER HEAD, $280, both by Czech & Speake, from Waterworks; 800-899-6757.

page 67

Antique marble shower BASEBOARD, $15 per linear foot, from Urban Archaeology, 285 Lafayette Street, New York, NY 10012; 212-431-6969. Custom glass-and-chrome SHOWER by Ketcham from Architectural Details International, 641 County Road 39A, Southampton, NY 11968; 516-283-7791. SHOWER HEAD, $280, by Czech & Speake, from Waterworks; 800-899-6757. LEAD TABLETOP, $125, from Sage Street Antiques, Sage Street and Route 114, Sag Harbor, NY 11963; 516-725-4036.

page 68

Chrome SOAP OVERTUB, $250, from Urban Archaeology, 285 Lafayette Street, New York, NY 10012; 212-431-6969.

pages 68 and 69

Wood PEDESTALS, $35, from Sage Street Antiques, Sage Street and Route 114, Sag Harbor, NY 11963; 516-725-4036.

page 69

19th-century HORN CUPS, from $48 to $150, from L. Becker Flowers, 217 East 83rd Street, New York, NY 10028; 212-439-6001. Giro Inglese HAND TOWEL, $55, from Anichini; 800-553-5309. French bronze doré WALL SCONCES from Consignmart, 877 Post Road East, Westport, CT 06880; 203-226-0841.

page 70

Top left: Belle Epoque SINK by Cesame, $1,975, from Waterworks; 800-899-6757. TOWEL BAR, SOAP HOLDER, and GLASS, all from Urban Archaeology, 285 Lafayette Street, New York, NY 10012; 212-431-6969. Top right: PORCELAIN TABLE from Urban Archaeology, see above. CHAIR, $45, from Sage Street Antiques, Sage Street and Route 114, Sag Harbor, NY 11963; 516-725-4036. Ironstone SOAP DISHES, $60 to

$65, from Vito Giallo Antiques, 222 East 83rd Street, New York, NY 10028; 212-535-9885. By appointment only. Bottom left: PINE MIRROR, $200 to $800, from Evergreen Antiques, 1249 Third Avenue, New York, NY 10021; 212-744-5664. Ironstone ICE-CREAM-MOLD SOAP DISH, $45, from Gordon Foster, 1322 Third Avenue, New York, NY 10021; 212-744-4922. Bottom right: China pedestal SINK from Sherle Wagner, 60 East 57th Street, New York, NY 10022; 212-758-3300.

page 71

Top right: Chrome double TOWEL BAR by Czech & Speake, $456, from Waterworks; 800-899-6757.

page 73

Cotton BATH TOWEL (used on chair) by Polo, $20, at Polo/Ralph Lauren stores; for information call 212-642-8700. Gray Belgian LINEN (used for piping and buttons), $32.95 per yard, from B & J Fabrics, 263 West 40th Street, New York, NY 10018; 212-354-8150.

page 75

Nickel-plated FAUCET by Czech & Speake, $895, from Waterworks; 800-899-6757. Custom HVAC half-inch LATTICE GRATE from Register and Grille Manufacturing, 202 Norman Avenue, Brooklyn, NY 11222; 718-383-9090. MEDICINE CABINET, $1,450, from Theron Ware Works of Art, 548 Warren Street, Hudson, NY 12534; 518-828-9744. Impero Spugna GUEST TOWEL, $20, from Anichini; 800-553-5309. MARBLE FLOOR by Joseph Corcoran Marble, 50 West Hills Road, Huntington Station, NY 11746; 516-423-8737. Duchess cashmere-and-merino queen-size BLANKET, $365, from Garnet Hill; 800-622-6216. Custom-made silk-charmeuse down-filled COMFORTER, by Stephen Balamut, from Allied Down Products, 84 Oak Street, Brooklyn, NY 11222; 718-389-5454. SILK CHARMEUSE, $22.95 per yard, from New York Elegant Fabrics, 240 West 40th Street, New York, NY 10018; 212-302-

4984. Cream flannel full flat SHEET and standard PILLOW SHAM, both by Purist, from ABC Carpet & Home, 888 Broadway, New York, NY 10003; 212-473-3000 or 800-888-7847.

pages 75 and 80
Raspberry WOOL CASHMERE, $82.95 per yard, from B & J Fabrics, 263 West 40th Street, New York, NY 10018; 212-354-8150. Pure & Simple all-cotton KNITTING YARN (color #5216) by Classic Elite, $5 per skein, from Crafts & Talk, 313 East 14th Street, New York, NY 10003; 212-777-5657.

page 76
Johnson and Wanzenberg artichoke TABLE LAMP, $550, from Fulper Glazes, P.O. BOX 373, Yardley, PA 19067; 215-736-8512. Tavern check FABRIC from Schumacher; call 800-332-3384 for nearest retailer.

page 77
French bamboo BED (c. 1890-1910) from Art Smith Antiques, Route 1, Wells Union Antiques, Wells, ME 04090; 207-646-6996. 19th-century English seltzer-bottle LAMPS, $2,100 for pair, from John Rosselli Antiques Ltd., 255 East 72nd Street, New York, NY 10021; 212-737-2739.

page 78
Custom-made matelassé cotton COVERLETS, about $150 for twin, from Touch of Europe, 135 Main Street, Westport, CT 06880; 203-227-3355.

LIGHT
page 82
Mahogany FLOOR LAMP from Ann-Morris Antiques, 239 East 60th Street, New York, NY 10022; 212-755-3308. To the trade only. TASSELS, $7 to $15, from M & J Trimming Co., 1008 Sixth Avenue, New York, NY 10018; 212-391-9072. 30" ACCENT LIGHT, $29.95, from the Lighting Center Ltd., 240 East 59th Street, New York, NY 10022; 212-888-8383.

page 85
Bronze Art Nouveau LAMP, $2,500, from Malmaison Antiques, 253 East 74th Street, New York, NY, 10021; 212-288-7861. 6"-by-

12"-by-9" PAPER LAMPSHADE, $27, from Just Shades, 21 Spring Street, New York, NY 10012; 212-966-2757.

page 86
Top left: Swing-arm brass SCONCE from Ann-Morris Antiques, 239 East 60th Street, New York, NY 10022; 212-755-3308. To the trade only. LAMPSHADE, $22, from Just Shades, 21 Spring Street, New York, NY 10012, 212-966-2757. Full-spectrum LIGHTBULBS from Duro-Test; call 800-289-3876 for nearest retailer. Also from Lumiram; call 800-354-5596 for nearest retailer. Top right: Polyester "Crepe de Stretch" LINING MATERIAL, $9 per yard, and custom-designed soft-lined SILK SHADE, both from Susanne Wellott/Shades from the Midnight Sun, 66 Boulder Trail, Bronxville, NY 10708; 914-779-7237. Khaki SILK CHARMEUSE, $24.95 per yard, from B & J Fabrics, 263 West 40th Street, New York, NY 10018; 212-354-8150. Early-20th-century mercury-glass LAMP BASE from Hubert des Forges, 1193 Lexington Avenue, New York, NY 10028; 212-744-1857). Bottom right: Mercury-glass candlestick LAMP, $475, from Hubert des Forges Antiques and Accessories, see above. Velvet LAMPSHADE by Susanne Wellott/Shades from the Midnight Sun, 66 Boulder Trail, Bronxville, NY 10708; 914-779-7237.

page 88
Mirrored sun SCONCE, $3,000, from John Rosselli International, 523 East 73rd Street, New York, NY 10021; 212-772-2137.

page 90
Cut-glass COLUMN LAMP, $450, from John Rosselli International, 523 East 73rd Street, New York, NY 10021; 212-772-2137.

WORKING
pages 92, 94 to 99
COUNTERS, CABINETS, SHELVES, DRAWERS, CARTS, and TABLES custom-made by Duralab Equipment Corp., 10723 Farragut Road, Brooklyn, NY 11236; 718-649-9600. (All Duralab products

are custom-ordered; there is no stock or inventory. Because pieces must be assembled, painted, and shipped, delivery may take some time.)

pages 92, 95 to 97
CARPENTRY by Ben Krupinski Builders, 15 Toilsome Lane, East Hampton, NY 11937; 516-324-3656.

page 92
Custom-made stainless-steel SHELVES from Klatt Sheet Metal, 479 Hubbard Avenue, Aquebogue, NY 11931; 516-722-3515. Gray FLOOR TILES by Astra (style #6006), $8.25 per square foot, white subway WALL TILES by H. & R. Johnson, $5 per square foot, and FAUCET (item #728-22), $150, all from Alan Court & Associates, 57B Main Street, East Hampton, NY 11937; 516-324-7497.

page 93
Fabric WALL COVERING from Ben Krupinski Builders, 15 Toilsome Lane, East Hampton, NY 11937; 516-324-3656. Laurel Haze FLOOR TILES by Astra (style #6004), $8.25 per square foot, from Alan Court & Associates, 57B Main Street, East Hampton, NY 11937; 516-324-7497. PIE-SAFE CUPBOARD, $325 to $525, from Nellie's of Amagansett, 255 Main Street, Amagansett, NY 11930; 516-267-1000. 1940s Shaw-Walker DESK CHAIR, $250, from 280 Modern, 280 Lafayette Street, New York, NY 10012; 212-941-5825. 1960s ceramic LAMP, $475, from David Stypmann, 192 Avenue of the Americas, New York, NY 10013; 212-226-5717. TOOL CART (#3160) (custom-painted Araucana Porcelain Green at an auto-body shop), $219.95, from Lyon Metal Products; 800-323-0082 for nearest retailer.

page 94
2-drawer FILE CABINET (custom-painted Araucana Porcelain Green at an auto-body shop), $174, from Sam Flax, 12 West 20th Street, New York, NY 10011; 212-620-3038.

page 96
White WOODEN BLINDS with white tapes custom-made by

Nanik, from Window Modes, 979 Third Avenue, New York, NY 10022; 212-752-1140.

pages 97 (top left) to 99
DESIGN by Richard Lewis, architect, 444 Central Park West, New York, NY 10025; 212-865-5661.

page 97
Aluminum CHAIRS, $195 each, from Chairs & Stools Etc., 222 Bowery, New York, NY 10012; 212-925-9191. White WOODEN BLINDS with white tapes custom-made by Nanik, from Window Modes, 979 Third Avenue, New York, NY 10022; 212-752-1140.

page 100
SWIVEL SLIDING SHELVES by Fulterer USA; 800-395-4646 for nearest dealer.

page 101
Nickel FAUCETS by Czech & Speake, $845 each, from Waterworks; 800-899-6757. Marble SINK (custom-made from separate pieces) from Joseph Corcoran Marble, 50 West Hills Road, Huntington Station, NY 11746; 516-423-8737.

page 102
ROOM DESIGN by Penny Fallmann May of May Architects, P.C., 1449 Lexington Avenue, New York, NY 10128; 212-534-2850. Circa 1930 mahogany reproduction CIRCLE-BACK CHAIR, $4,200, from Mariette Himes Gomez Associates, 506 East 74th Street, New York, NY 10021; 212-288-6856. Pairot iron TRIPOD TABLE BASE from Paula Rubenstein Antiques, 65 Prince Street, New York, NY 10012; 212-966-8954.

page 103
Cherry TELEPHONE STAND by Matthew Smyth, $1,800, from Mrs. MacDougall, 979 Third Avenue, New York, NY 10022; 212-688-7754.

page 104
Circa 1880 folding iron LOUNGE CHAIR, $2,600, from Historical Materialism, 125 Crosby Street, New York, NY 10012; 212-431-3424. Parramore Island STRIPED FABRIC for cushion (in Parramore Red), $88.50 per yard, from Rogers & Goffigon, 979 Third Avenue, New York, NY 10022;

212-888-3242. CHENILLE BLANKET
(#1735778), RUG, and CHILD'S
CHAIR (#1516848), all from ABC
Carpet & Home, 888 Broadway,
New York, NY 10003;
212-473-3000 or 800-888-7847.

pages 105 and 106
Steel restaurant TABLE, $195,
from Leader Restaurant
Equipment & Supplies, 191
Bowery, New York, NY 10002;
212-677-1982. Metal CABINET
from Ruby Beets, Montauk
Highway, Bridgehampton, NY
11962; 516-537-2802. Mailing
address: Box 596, Wainscott, NY
11975. FILE BOXES, $4.75 each,
from Light Impressions; 800-828-
6216. C File TABLE by Icon
Design Studios, 338 West 49th
Street, New York, NY 10019; 212-
581-8529. Moppe BOXES, $15,
Muck FILE BOXES, $9 each, and
Arcus WINDOW SHADES, $12, all
from IKEA; 800-434-4532 for East
Coast retail information, 800-899-
4532 for West Coast locations.
PILLOW (#1965201), from ABC
Carpet & Home, 888 Broadway,
New York, NY 10003; 212-473-
3000 or 800-888-7847. DESK LAMP
by Luxo (#18-5052), $149, from
Charrette; 800-367-3729 for store
locations. METAL BOXES, $45
each, from Historical Materialism,
125 Crosby Street, New York, NY
10012; 212-431-3424.

page 107
Cube Mate STORAGE COMPART-
MENTS, $54, from Sam Flax, 12
West 20th Street, New York, NY
10011; 212-620-3038. Used OFFICE
CHAIR, $25, from Allen Office
Furniture, 165 West 23rd Street,
New York, NY 10011; 212-741-
3385. FABRIC covering chair by
Donghia (Plante d'Hiver #3320)
from Donghia Textiles, 485
Broadway, New York, NY 10013;
212-925-2777 or 800-366-4442.
Costanzina TABLE LAMP, $168,
from Lee's Studio, 1755
Broadway, New York, NY 10019;
212-247-0110. Circa 1945 saddle-
stitched leather DESK BLOTTER,
$300, Robert Janssen gelatin silver
PRINT, $845, and c. 1933
Emanuel Weil chlorobromide
PRINT "Plant Study," $2,340, all
from AERO Ltd., 132 Spring

Street, New York, NY 10012;
212-966-1500. Round Russian
birch-bark BOXES, $20 TO $50,
from William Lipton, Ltd., 27
East 61st Street, New York, NY
10021; 212-751-8131. Small
STRAW BOX (for computer disks),
$10, from Be Seated, 66
Greenwich Avenue, New York,
NY 10011; 212-924-8444. Terra-
cotta CARDBOARD STORAGE
BOX, $20, from Mxyplyzyk, 125
Greenwich Avenue, New York,
NY 10014; 212-989-4300. Custom-
made WOODEN SUPPLY BOXES
by Icon Design Studios, 338 West
49th Street, New York, NY
10019; 212-581-8529. GALVANIZED-
METAL BOX, $9, from IKEA; call
800-434-4532 for East Coast retail
information or 800-899-4532 for
West Coast locations. Unfinished
oval SHAKER BOX, $46.75, from
Shaker Workshop, P.O. BOX 8001,
Ashburnham, MA 01430;
617-646-8985.

page 108
Metal DISK BOX, $45, from Sam
Flax, 12 West 20th Street, New
York, NY 10011; 212-620-3038.
FILE CABINET, $1,220, from
Haller Systems, 150 East 58th
Street, New York, NY 10155;
212-371-1230. Cashmere FELT
PADS sewn by Ann Sison, 131
East 83rd Street, New York, NY
10028; 212-249-8213.

page 109
ROOM DESIGN by Walter
Chatham Architects, 580
Broadway, Room 1001, New
York, NY 10012; 212-925-2202.
CABINET WORK by C.N.M.
Construction Co., 67-23 Main
Street, Flushing, NY 11367;
212-764-0403. Hanging CEILING
LANTERN, $450, from Ten Eyck-
Emerich Antiques, 342 Pequot
Avenue, Southport, CT 06490;
203-259-2559. Siena Giallo MAR-
BLE FLOORING from Joseph
Corcoran Marble, 50 West Hills
Road, Huntington Station, NY
11746; 516-423-8737. CANE OCCA-
SIONAL CHAIR from Bielecky
Brothers, 306 East 61st Street,
New York, NY 10021; 212-753-
2355. To the trade only. 1930s
French DESK LAMP, $600, from
Wyeth, 151 Franklin Street, New

York, NY 10013; 212-925-5278.
Korean SILVER TOBACCO BOX,
$1,575, from William Lipton Ltd.,
27 East 61st Street, New York,
NY 10021; 212-751-8131.

WALLS
page 110
Schreuder SWEDISH PUTTY, $25
for 1 kg, $75 for 5 kg (tinting $15
per 5 kg), from Fine Paints of
Europe, Box 419, Woodstock, VT
05091; 800-332-1556. Folding
limed-oak SCREEN, c. 1940,
$4,200, Hanson chrome LAMP,
$695, and aluminum-leaf BENCH,
$985, all from AERO Ltd., 132
Spring Street, New York, NY
10012; 212-966-1500.

pages 110 and 113
Fortuny hand-painted silk HANG-
ING FIXTURE, $1,950, from
Distant Origin, 153 Mercer
Street, New York, NY 10012;
212-941-0024.

page 113
19th-century French gold-leaf
MIRROR, $2,500, from Amy
Perlin Antiques, 1020 Lexington
Avenue, New York, NY 10021;
212-744-4923.

page 114
Stick-and-ball spool TABLE, $400,
and Victorian PRESSED FERNS
ON PAPER, both from Ruby
Beets, Montauk Highway,
Bridgehampton, NY; 516-537-2802.
Mailing address: Box 596,
Wainscott, NY 11975.

page 116
Top left: PICTURE FRAMES and
CUSTOM-CUT MATS, $25 and up
depending on size, both from
Skyframe, 96 Spring Street, New
York, NY 10012; 212-226-6026.
Top right: All PAINT from
Benjamin Moore: wall, #925;
trim, mixed from #492; ceiling,
mixed from #631; floor, blue
porch-and-floor enamel. Bottom:
base wall, #925; blue panel,
#745; trim, white eggshell finish;
ceiling, #932. Call 800-826-2623
for nearest retailer.

page 118
All PAINT from Benjamin Moore:
base wall, mixed from #526;
panel, #536; trim and ceiling,
#904. Call 800-826-2623 for near-
est retailer.

page 119
Brass ANDIRONS, $495, at
American Folk Art Gallery, 374
Bleecker Street, New York, NY
10014; 212-366-6566. All PAINT
from Benjamin Moore: base wall,
#925; pink stripes, mixed from
#093; mantel, #904; baseboard,
#940 semigloss; cornice, #940
flat; ceiling, Superwhite flat. Call
800-826-2623 for nearest retailer.

page 120
PUTTY FINISHING by Jesse
Krzywon of C. N. Renovation,
1167 McBride Avenue, West
Paterson, NJ 07424; 201-890-9898.
Schreuder Swedish PUTTY, $25
for 1 kg, $75 for 5 kg (tinting $15
per 5 kg), available from Fine
Paints of Europe, Box 419, Wood-
stock, VT 05091; 800-332-1556.

RELAXING
pages 123 to 126
All PILLOWS, CUSHIONS, BOL-
STERS, and PADS sewn by Ann
Baderian Polokoff Ltd.; 35-38
164th Street, Flushing, NY 11358;
718-359-0309.

page 123
Sunbrella FABRIC IN VANILLA
(#4629), $11.50 per yard (47"),
from Action Awning & Sign
Corp., 40-28 24th Street, Long
Island City, NY 11101; 800-464-
7818. Giati Textiles MONTAGE
COLLECTION FABRIC (Rose
Blush, #804) and SUNFAST FAB-
RIC (Peach Petal, #1012), both
$47 per yard, from Giati Designs,
614 Santa Barbara Street, Santa
Barbara, CA 93130; 805-965-6535.
To the trade only; call for local
showroom.

pages 124 and 125
Sunbrella YELLOW-AND-WHITE-
STRIPED FABRIC (Fancy, #4794),
$11.50 per yard (47"), from Action
Awning & Sign Corp.; 800-464-
7818. Giati Textiles Sunfast BLUE-
AND-WHITE-STRIPED FABRIC
(Admiral Field, #056), $47 per
yard, from Giati Designs, 614
Santa Barbara Street, Santa
Barbara, CA 93130; 805-965-6535.
To the trade only; call for local
showroom. BLUE-AND-YELLOW-
STRIPED FABRIC (Charlotte
Tournesol #4362/26), from
Manuel Canovas, 979 Third

Avenue, New York, NY 10022; 212-752-9588. To the trade only. Giati Textiles Sunfast YELLOW-AND-WHITE TENT-STRIPED FABRIC (Tent Yellow, #025), $47 per yard, from Giati Designs, see above. Blue-and-white-striped UMBRELLA (CW109MB) and black STEEL BASE (MB111BB), both from Dayva International, 7642 Windfield Drive, Huntington Beach, CA 92647; 714-842-9697. To the trade only.

page 126
Giati Textiles Sunfast GREEN-AND-WHITE STRIPED FABRIC (Polo Field, #030), $47 per yard; Giati Textiles Sunfast GREEN-AND-WHITE TENT-STRIPED FABRIC (Tent Polo, #049), $47 per yard; both from Giati Designs, 614 Santa Barbara Street, Santa Barbara, CA 93130; 805-965-6535. To the trade only; call for local showroom. White CAFÉ CHAIRS, $89 for set of 2, from Gardeners Eden; 800-822-9600.

page 127
Giati Textiles SUNFAST FABRIC (Laguna Blue, #009), $47 per yard, from Giati Designs, 614 Santa Barbara Street, Santa Barbara, CA 93130; 805-965-6535. To the trade only; call for local showroom. Sunbrella FABRIC IN OYSTER (#4642), $11.50 per yard (47"), from Action Awning & Sign Corp., 40-28 24th Street, Long Island City, NY 11101; 800-464-7818. VINTAGE PATTERNED FABRIC (on pillows), prices vary, from Paula Rubenstein Ltd., 65 Prince Street, New York, NY 10012; 212-966-8954. Giati Textiles Westhampton Collection all-cotton CANVAS in natural (#101), $40 per yard, from Giati Designs, 614 Santa Barbara Street, Santa Barbara, CA 93130; 805-965-6535. To the trade only; call for local showroom.

pages 130 and 131
Aluminum CHAIRS, $195 each, from Chairs & Stools Etc., 222 Bowery, New York, NY 10012; 212-925-9191. ANTIQUE JARS (used as candle holders), $125 to $225, from Evergreen Antiques, 1249 Third Avenue, New York, NY 10021; 212-744-5664.

page 133
French CAFÉ CHAIRS (at table), $450 to $850, from T & K French Antiques, 200 Lexington Avenue, Suite 202, New York, NY 10016; 212-219-2472. InterMetro custom stainless-steel SHELVING, from New York Store Fixture Co., 167 Bowery, New York, NY 10002; 212-226-0044 or 800-336-8353.

page 135
UNTITLED WORK ON PAPER by David Carrino; 212-473-0249 for similar works.

pages 136 and 138
5'-by-10' CANVAS PANELS (Sunbrella/Natural #4604, $15.35 for 47") from C. E. King & Sons, 10 St. Francis Place, East Hampton, NY 11937; 516-324-4944.

pages 137 and 139
2'-by-12' POLYESTER-MESH PANELS (Textilene Sunsure, style #10-7126, $13 per yard) from C. E. King & Sons, 10 St. Francis Place, East Hampton, NY 11937; 516-324-4944.

FLOORS
page 140
All PAINT from Benjamin Moore: Prescott Green (#HC140), Hollingsworth Green (#HC141), Woodland Blue (#HC147), and Yarmouth Blue (#HC150), 800-826-2623 for nearest retailer. TASK LIGHT (LB2A with an E base), $186 from Luxo Corp., 36 Midland Avenue, Port Chester, NY 10573; 800-222-5896. Free catalog. Stacking STORAGE CUBES, $30 each, from Hold Everything; 800-421-2264. Free catalog. Storsund CHAIR, $99, from IKEA; call 800-434-4532 for East Coast retail information, 800-899-4532 for West Coast locations.

pages 144 and 145
Late-19th-century English INGRAIN CARPET, $28,000, and 19th-century BORDERED ENGLISH INGRAIN CARPET, $12,500, from Beauvais Carpets, 201 East 57th Street, New York, NY 10022; 212-688-2265.

pages 146 and 150
BASE FLOOR PAINT Silver Lining (#2288), and GLAZING LIQUID by

Pratt & Lambert; 800-289-7728 for nearest retailer. UNIVERSAL TINTS, by Valspar; 800-767-2532 for nearest retailer. Diamond Finish SATIN SEALER by Varathane; 800-635-3286 for nearest retailer.

page 146
Odenslunda CHAIRS, $250 each, from IKEA; 800-434-4532 for East Coast retail locations or 800-899-4532 for West Coast locations. Brass-leaf ANDIRONS by Drenttel Doyle Projects. To the trade only, through John Boone, 1059 Third Avenue, New York, NY 10021; 212-758-0012; and J. Robert Scott, 8727 Melrose Avenue, Los Angeles, CA 90069; 310-659-4910. Pine DEMI-LUNE TABLES, c. 1830, $2,100 per pair, from Evergreen Antiques, 1249 Third Avenue, New York, NY 10021; 212-744-5664.

pages 147 and 151
BASE PAINT Osprey (#1292) and GLAZING LIQUID by Pratt & Lambert; 800-289-7728 for nearest retailer. UNIVERSAL TINTS by Valspar; 800-767-2532 for nearest retailer. Diamond Finish SATIN SEALER by Varathane; 800-635-3286 for nearest retailer.

page 148
Laurel Haze cement glazed FLOOR TILES by Astra (style #6004), $8.25 per square foot, from Alan Court & Associates, 57B Main Street, East Hampton, NY 11937; 516-324-7497.

page 151
UNIVERSAL TINTS by Valspar; 800-767-2532 for nearest retailer. GRAINING ROLLER and RUBBER COMB, $20 to $25, both from Fine Paints of Europe, Box 419, Woodstock, VT 05091; 800-332-1556.

GINGHAM PATTERN TEMPLATES

Use these templates along with the directions on page 150 to create the painted gingham floor shown on page 146. For ease of use, you might want to photocopy and enlarge the templates.

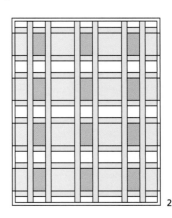
1

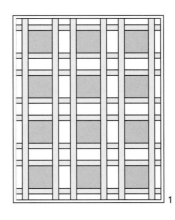
2

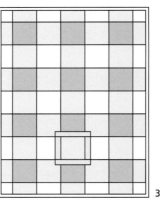
3

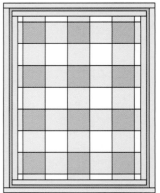
4

Index

If you have enjoyed reading
and using THE BEST OF
MARTHA STEWART LIVING:
HOW TO DECORATE,
please join us as a subscriber
to MARTHA STEWART LIVING,
the magazine.
Simply call toll-free
800-999-6518.
The annual subscription rate
is $24 for 10 issues.

Credits

BIBLIOGRAPHY

Abercrombie, Stanley. *A Philosophy of Interior Design* (New York: Icon Editions/Harper & Row, 1990).

Calloway, Stephen. *Twentieth-Century Decoration* (New York: Harry N. Abrams, 1989).

————, general editor, and Elizabeth Cromley, consultant editor. *The Elements of Style* (New York: Simon and Schuster, 1991).

Gere, Charlotte. *Ninetheenth-Century Decoration/ The Art of the Interior* (New York: Rizzoli International Publications, Inc., 1988).

Pile, John F. *Interior Design,* Second Edition (New York: Harry N. Abrams, 1995).

Praz, Mario. *An Illustrated History of Interior Decoration: From Pompeii to Art Nouveau* (New York: Thames and Hudson, 1994).

Rybczynski, Witold. *Home: A Short History of an Idea* (New York: Penguin Books, 1987).

Thornton, Peter. *Authentic Decor: The Domestic Interior 1620-1920* (New York: Crescent Books, 1993).

Wharton, Edith, and Ogden Codman, Jr. *The Decoration of Houses* (New York: W.W. Norton & Co., 1978).

PHOTOGRAPHY AND ILLUSTRATION

William Abranowicz	32-39, 44, 56 (all but top left), 57, 61-63, 73, 75, 80, 81 (left), 82, 85, 86 (top left and right), 87-99, 102-109, 122-127, 136-139, 144-145, back cover (top center, bottom center and right)
Ruvén Afanador	page 86 (bottom left and top right)
Michel Arnaud	pages 42, 43
Harry Bates	page 80
Carlton Davis	page 86 (bottom right), 116 (top left)
John Dugdale	page 115
Todd Eberle	front cover
Gentl & Hyers	pages 72 (left), 128-129
Thibault Jeanson	pages 2-4, 6, 8, 12, 13, 16-19, 21, 22, 23 (top left and bottom right), 24 (top left), 26, 40, 41, 45-50, 53-55, 56 (top left), 58-60, 64, 65, 70 (bottom left), 76-78, 100-101, 110, 113-114, 117, 120, 130-135, 140, 143, 146-151, back cover (top left and right, center left, bottom left)
Stephen Lewis	pages 79, 81 (right)
Tom McWilliams	page 29
Maria Robledo	page 5
Bruce Wolf	pages 10, 15, 20, 23 (top right and bottom left), 24 (top right and bottom left, 25, 27, 30, 66-70 (all but bottom left,) 71, 72 (right), 74, 75 (left), 116 (top right and bottom left), 118, 119, 121

EXECUTIVE EDITOR
Carol Kramer

ART DIRECTION
Claudia Bruno, Helen Delany, Agnethe Glatved, Laura Harrigan, Anne Johnson, Anne-Marie Midy, Eric A. Pike, Constance Old, Scot Schy, Gael Towey, Jennifer Waverek

STYLISTS
Eve Ashcraft, Anita Calero, Calvin Churchman, Stephen Earle, Necy Fernandes, Tom Flynn, Fritz Karch, David McLean, Hannah Milman, Kathy Oberman, Lisa Wagner

PHOTO EDITING
Heidi J. Posner, Kevin Guterl

DESIGN PRODUCTION
Paula Blum, Michelle DiCicco

PUBLISHING
Lauren Podlach Stanich, Rich Fontaine, Alisa Kigner

PRODUCTION
Dora Braschi Cardinale, George D. Planding, Nicole M. Lobisco

PRINTING
Ernest V. Cardinale of Satellite Graphics, Myra Tiller and Linda Campbell of Quebecor Printing